Conference Proceedings of the Society for Experimental Mechanics Series

Series Editor

Kristin B. Zimmerman
Society for Experimental Mechanics, Inc.,
Bethel, USA

The Conference Proceedings of the Society for Experimental Mechanics Series presents early findings and case studies from a wide range of fundamental and applied work across the broad range of fields that comprise Experimental Mechanics. Series volumes follow the principle tracks or focus topics featured in each of the Society's two annual conferences: IMAC, A Conference and Exposition on Structural Dynamics, and the Society's Annual Conference & Exposition and will address critical areas of interest to researchers and design engineers working in all areas of Structural Dynamics, Solid Mechanics and Materials Research.

Chi-Hung Hwang • Gordon Shaw • Motoharu Fujigaki
Editors

Advancement of Optical Methods & Digital Image Correlation in Experimental Mechanics, Vol. 2

Proceedings of the 2025 Annual Conference on Experimental and Applied Mechanics

River Publishers

Published, sold and distributed by:

River Publishers
Broagervej 10
9260 Gistrup
Denmark

www.riverpublishers.com

ISBN 97887-438-0828-2 (Hardback)

ISBN 97887-438-0833-6 (eBook)

https://doi.org/10.13052/9788743808282

Conference Proceedings of the Society for Experimental Mechanics

An imprint of River Publishers

Preface

Advancement of Optical Methods & Digital Image Correlation in Experimental Mechanics represents one of five volumes of technical papers presented at the SEM 2025 SEM Annual Conference & Exposition on Experimental and Applied Mechanics organized by the Society for Experimental Mechanics and held in Milwaukee, WI, June 2-5, 2025. The complete Proceedings also includes volumes on: *Dynamic Behavior of Materials; Mechanics of Biological Systems and Materials and the Mechanics of Composite, Hybrid & Multifunctional Materials; Fracture, Fatigue, Failure, Damage Evolution and Thermomechanics & Infrared Imaging; and Mechanics of Additive & Advanced Manufacturing, Inverse Methods and Machine Learning.*

Each collection presents early findings from experimental and computational investigations on an important area within Experimental Mechanics, Optical Methods & Digital Image Correlation (DIC) being important areas.

With the advancement in imaging instrumentation, lighting resources, computational power, metrology and data storage, optical methods have gained wide application throughout the experimental mechanics community during the past decades. These methods have been applied for measurements over a wide range of spatial domains and temporal resolution. Optical methods have used a full range of wavelengths from X-Ray to visible lights and infrared. They have been developed not only to make two-dimensional and three-dimensional deformation measurements on surfaces, but also to make volumetric measurements throughout the interior of a material body.

The areas of Digital Image Correlation (DIC) and Digital Volume Correlation (DVC) have been an integral track within the SEM Annual Conference, spearheaded by Professor Michael Sutton from the University of South Carolina. The contributed papers within this section of the volume span technical aspects of DIC and DVC.

In addition, papers were contributed to celebrate Prof. Fu-Pen Chiang's retirement from Stonybrook University.

The conference organizers thank the authors, presenters, and session chairs for their participation, support, and contribution to this very exciting area of experimental mechanics.

Editors:
Chi-Hung Hwang-*Taiwan Instrument Technology Research Center, Taiwan;* Gordon Shaw, *National Institute of Standards and Technology, MD, USA; Motoharu Fujigaki, University of Fukui, Fukui, Japan*

Contents

1 **Experimental and Numerical Analysis of Buckling in Welded Rail Systems** 1
Ganesh Ramaswamy, K. Ramesh, and U. Saravanan

2 **An in-situ Grain-resolved Study of FCC Nickel Plasticity over Gross Granular Fields using Digital Image Correlation with High Resolution Optical Microscopy** 5
Olcay Türkoğlu and C. Can Aydıner

3 **Residual Stress Evaluation in Silicon Wafer Based on the Principle of Superposition and Full-Field Warpage Measurement** 13
Satoru Yoneyama, Keisuke Iizuka, and Mitsuaki Kudo

4 **GPU-Accelerated Triangulation in the Stereo-DIC Algorithm Using a Heterogeneous Framework** 17
Mullai Thiagu, Rupesh Nasre, and Sankara J. Subramanian

5 **A Sublimation-based Pattern Generation Technique for Deformation Analysis of Additively Manufactured Specimens** 27
Nicolas A. Yusim, Angel Matos-De Los Santos, Austin M. Giordano, and Fu-Pen Chiang

6 **Deformation Measurement of Structure Using Sampling Moire Method with SfM-MVS** 33
Shohei Itakura and Motoharu Fujigaki

7 **Development of an *in-situ* Sensor for Real-time Geometrical Inspection in Additive Manufacturing** 39
Howard Zheng, Anthony Salerni and Cosme Furlong

8 **Development of Mixed Reality Methods for Immersive Visualization of 3D Dynamic Optical Testing Measurements** 47
Daniel Ruiz-Cadalso, Lorena Maria Genua, Jonathan Oliveira Luiz, Cosme Furlong, Lee Moradi, and Vladimir Vantsevich

9 **Development of an Instantaneous Phase-shifting Lensless Digital Holographic Otoscope for Quantitative Imaging of the Human Eardrum *in-vivo*** 53
Daniel Ruiz-Cadalso, Jonathan O. Luiz, Jeffrey T. Cheng, and Cosme Furlong

Chapter 1
Experimental and Numerical Analysis of Buckling in Welded Rail Systems

Ganesh Ramaswamy, K. Ramesh, and U. Saravanan

Abstract Modern rail networks are increasingly adopting welded rail systems over jointed rails due to better rider comfort. Welding restricts free expansion of rails due to ambient temperature change. Rail Neutral Temperature (RNT) refers to that temperature at which welded rails are stress-free. Hence, at any given rail temperature above RNT, the rails experience a compressive stress build-up due to restricted strains. This can precipitate buckling of the rails thereby compromising safety and there is a need to study this closely. Multiple factors such as rail imperfections, fastener stiffness, ballast lateral stiffness and vehicular loads influence the phenomenon of rail buckling. Given that field tests to study this problem are cumbersome and cost-intensive, simplified model studies are desirable for understanding the influence and interaction between these contributing factors alongside validated numerical models. Towards this, model experiments are carried out using 3D printed rails. The sleeper systems are fabricated using filament-based printing and polyurethane is used to simulate the lateral supports offered by the ballast bed. A jig is designed to achieve the load application with the required end support conditions in the experiment. The system level response including the mobilization of lateral resistance offered by ballast bed is studied using transmission photoelasticity. The key connection identified using photoelasticity is studied for effect of fastener failure on lateral displacement using digital image correlation. The results from a finite element simulation are compared with experimental results to bring out the need for refinement. This study showcases the utility of simple model experiments to identify critical parameters and combinations that influence rail buckling which can be further used to refine numerical models. The knowledge acquired using cost-effective model experiments can also help guide field tests to better understand the problem of rail instability.

Keywords Photoelasticity · DIC · CWR Buckling · RNT · Instability

Introduction

Welded rails are widely adopted over jointed rails due to enhanced rider comfort. However, welding restricts the free expansion of rails due to ambient temperature changes and causes thermal stress build-up. Rail Neutral Temperature (RNT) is a crucial factor in determining the stress state of welded rails. At low temperatures, the rails are subjected to tension which poses the risk of rail fracture. However, when rail temperature exceeds RNT, compressive stress builds up, potentially leading to rail buckling and compromising safety. Multiple factors such as rail imperfections, fastener stiffness, ballast lateral stiffness, and vehicular loads influence rail buckling [1]. Researchers have attempted to study the problem using analytical methods [2, 3] as well as numerical models [1, 4]. While these can be helpful in studying the problem, experimental information is often invaluable for validating the idealizations involved. Data from multiple field tests have been reported in literature [2, 5] and researchers have also attempted to study the problem using prototype experiments [6] for ballastless

Ganesh Ramaswamy · K. Ramesh
Department of Applied Mechanics and Biomedical Engineering,
Indian Institute of Technology Madras, Chennai, India - 600036
e-mail: ganeshrvenkatraman@gmail.com; kramesh@zmail.iitm.ac.in

U. Saravanan
Department of Civil Engineering,
Indian Institute of Technology Madras, Chennai, India - 600036
e-mail: saran@zmail.iitm.ac.in

Chi-Hung Hwang et al. (eds.), *Advancement of Optical Methods & Digital Image Correlation in Experimental Mechanics, Vol. 2*, Conference Proceedings
of the Society for Experimental Mechanics Series, https://doi.org/10.13052/9788743808282-1

tracks. Given the challenges associated with such cost-intensive testing, simplified model studies that can complement such analyses are desirable for developing better understanding. Model experiments have been used previously to understand welded rail fracture [7]. In this work, an experimental study is carried out using a scaled down model of a track system with rails and sleepers alongside numerical modelling. The experimental technique of photoelasticity is used to examine the mobilization of lateral resistance and digital image correlation is used to study the effect of fastener failure on the lateral displacement at a connection. The result for this case from a finite element model developed in Abaqus® is compared with the experimental results to understand certain shortcomings and the need for further refinement.

Experimetal setup

An experimental jig is designed and fabricated in order to study the problem using scaled down models. Geometric similarity is used with a scale factor of 14.35. Standard gauge is considered for scaling down the transverse spacing of the rails which is maintained at 100 mm centres along with a sleeper spacing of 45 mm centres. The models are made using fused deposition modeling based printing using an Anycubic Kobra 2 Neo 3D printer. The rail is printed using premium thermoplastic polyurethane (TPU) with a shore hardness rating of 95A and the sleeper models are made using Polylactide acid thermoplastic (PLA). The connection between the rail and the sleeper is simulated using fasteners with toe load controlled using Duratool adjustable torque wrench with a uniform tightening of 0.1 Nm maintained at all connections. The lateral support offered by the ballast bed is simulated using high quality polyurethane strips in order to study the mobilization of lateral reactions. The end conditions are controlled using end plates which arrest translation and rotation in order to analyze the middle third of a considered buckled track length of 10 m which is close to values reported in literature [8]. A finite element (FE) model is parallelly developed in Abaqus® using axial connectors and springs to simulate the rail-track system response. The schematic of a representative model and the finite element model is shown in Fig. 1.

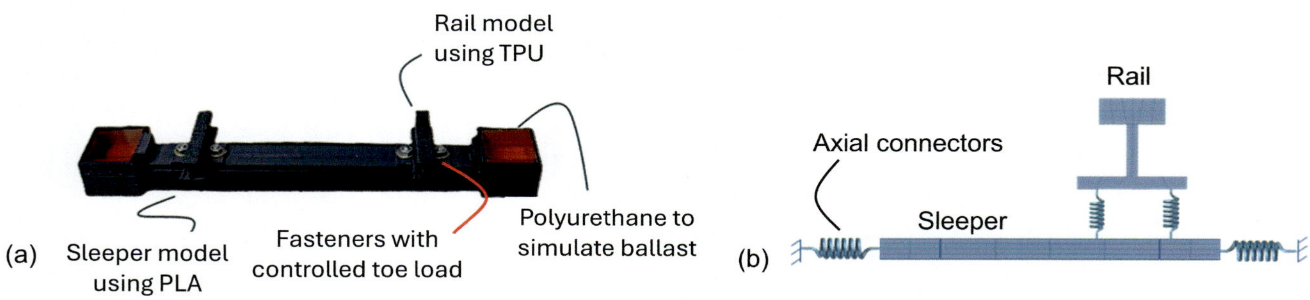

Fig. 1 (a) A representative scaled down experimental model of track system and (b) finite element model of rail and sleeper

Results and Discussion

Ballast offers lateral resistance to the sleeper systems to arrest in-plane movement of the welded rail track and the magnitude of this resistance is affected by changes in factors such as packing density, track alignment, etc. In this study, ballast action is simulated using transparent polyurethane which is photoelastically highly sensitive and exhibits stress-induced birefringence [9]. Hence, any minor deviations in the resistance offered can be identified by placing the setup in a polariscope and observing the photoelastic fringes as shown in Fig. 2

It is observed that resistance is mobilized in a slightly asymmetric manner when there is no compression applied (Fig. 2 b) which can be attributed to out-of-straightness of the rails and sleeper system. Further, when full compression is introduced, the right-side top (Fig. 2 c) shows a higher response indicating the tendency of the system to buckle. Buckling of CWRs can be at a system level as well as a local distortion which can contribute to flange climbing of wheelsets. The latter is more dangerous since it cannot be easily identified. Failure of rail-sleeper fasteners can aggravate this problem when the rail is subjected to high compression. Hence, it is of interest to examine the effect of fastener failure on the lateral displacement of the rails. Towards this, two sets of experiments are conducted using the technique of digital image correlation to evaluate the lateral displacement of the rail with and without fasteners. The critical connection to examine is chosen based on the lateral

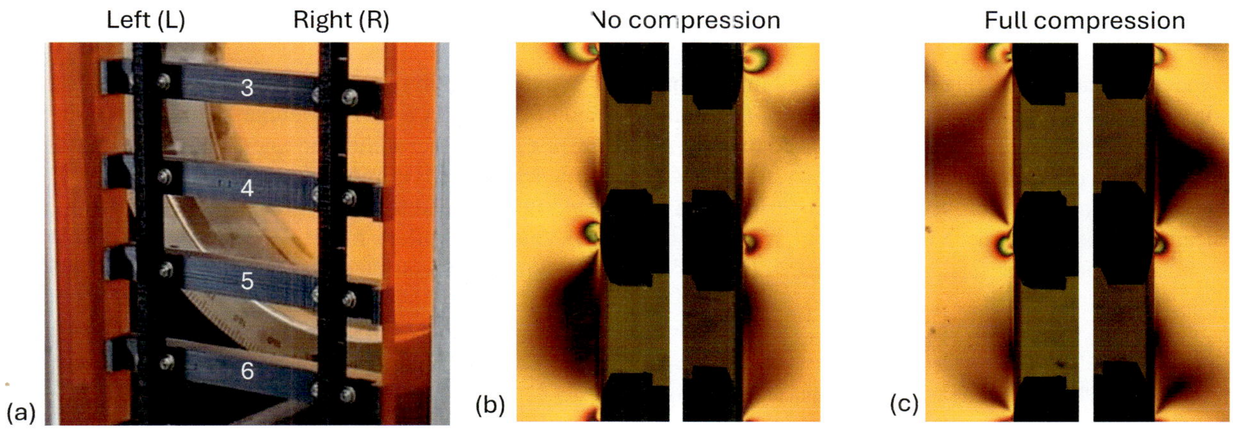

Fig. 2 (a) Model experimental setup placed in a polariscope with right and left rail indicated; photoelastic fringes on left and right at three sleeper levels 3-5 with (b) no compression and (c) full compression applied on the rails

mobilized reaction observed from photoelasticity (Fig. 2 c) and the processed results along with a displacement plot from the numerical model are presented in Fig. 3.

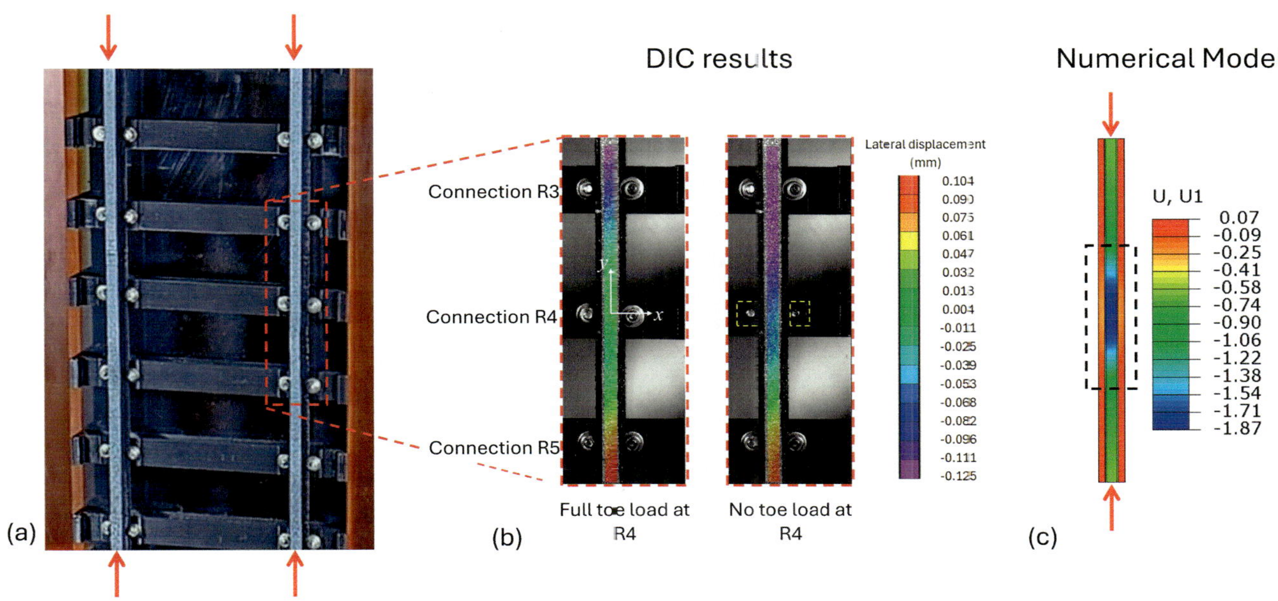

Fig. 3 (a) Loaded model with connections R3 to R5 considered for examining fastener failure, (b) DIC results for full toe load and no toe load at connection R4 and (c) displacement plot from finite element model with no fastener in the middle

It is observed from Fig. 3 b that the lateral displacement gets modified at connection R4 when the fastener is removed. This indicates that such a failure becomes crucial in high temperature conditions when the compressive stress build-up is high. The resulting local distortion of the rail may precipitate derailment by flange climbing. A comparison of the relative lateral displacement from the finite element model shows qualitative match at the connection where the fastener fails (Fig. 3 c). However, at other connections, the nature of displacements show deviations which could be attributed to the absence of local imperfections in the finite element model. Hence, comparisons with experimental results can help refine the idealizations in the finite element model in order to obtain predictions closer to the actual behaviour of welded rails.

Conclusion

This study integrates photoelasticity and digital image correlation to study buckling of welded rails using scaled-down model experiments with components fabricated using FDM printing. Photoelasticity is used to examine the mobilization of lateral resistance and digital image correlation is used to bring out the effect of fastener failure on lateral displacement of rails. A finite element model is developed in Abaqus® and the result of fastener failure is compared with experiments which show a similar behavior at the failure location. The comparison also highlights the need to refine the model by including local and global imperfections in order to obtain more reliable predictions. This study offers some insights into rail buckling using cost-effective model experiments and can be helpful in guiding design of large-scale field studies aimed at improving rail stability.

Acknowledgments The first author would like to thankfully acknowledge the discussions and support extended by Mr. Anand C and Mr. Shins K from the Digital Photomechanics Group at the Indian Institute of Technology Madras.

References

1. I. Villalba, R. Insa, P. Salvador, and P. Martinez, "Methodology for evaluating thermal track buckling in dual gauge tracks with continuous welded rail," *Proc Inst Mech Eng F J Rail Rapid Transit*, vol. 231, no. 3, pp. 269–279, 2017, doi:10.1177/0954409715626957.
2. A. D. Kerr, "Lateral Buckling Of Railroad Tracks Due To Constrained Thermal Expansions — A Critical Survey," *Railroad Track Mechanics and Technology*, pp. 141–169, Jan. 1978, doi:10.1016/B978-0-08-021923-3.50013-9.
3. A. D. Kerr, "Determination of Admissible Temperature Increases to Prevent Vertical Track Buckling," *ASME*, vol. 45, no. September 1978, https://doi.org/10.1115/1.3424362
4. N. H. Lim, S. Y. Han, T. H. Han, and Y. J. Kang, "Parametric Study on Stability of Continuous Welded Rail Track - Ballast Resistance and Track Irregularity," *International Journal of Steel Structures*, vol. 8, no. 3, pp. 171–181, 2008.
5. N. Hasan, "Thermal buckling of ballasted tangent track," *Advances in Mechanical Engineering*, vol. 12, no. 10, pp. 1–11, 2020, doi: 10.1177/1687814020968992.
6. C. Kang, M. Bode, M. Wenner, and S. Marx, "Experimental and numerical investigations of rail behaviour under compressive force on ballastless track systems," *Eng Struct*, vol. 197, Oct. 2019, doi: 10.1016/j.engstruct.2019.109413.
7. G. Ramaswamy, N. Verma, U. Saravanan, and K. Ramesh, "Criticality of Cracks in Rails Using Photoelasticity and Finite Elements," in *Advancement of Optical Methods and Fracture and Fatigue, Volume 3*, C. Furlong, C.-H. Hwang, G. Shaw, R. Berke, G. Pataky, and S. Hutchens, Eds., Cham: Springer Nature Switzerland, 2024, pp. 85–88, https://doi.org/10.1007/978-3-031-50499-0_14
8. C. Ngamkhanong, C. M. Wey, and S. Kaewunruen, "Buckling Analysis of Interspersed Railway Tracks," *Applied Sciences*, vol. 10, no. 9, p. 3091, Apr. 2020, doi: 10.3390/app10093091.
9. K. Ramesh, *Developments in Photoelasticity A renaissance*. IOP Publishing, 2021, https://doi.org/10.1088/978-0-7503-2472-4

Chapter 2
An in-situ Grain-resolved Study of FCC Nickel Plasticity over Gross Granular Fields using Digital Image Correlation with High Resolution Optical Microscopy

Olcay Türkoğlu and C. Can Aydıner

Abstract A recent implementation (Türkoğlu, O., Aydıner, C., *Exp Mech* **64**: 655–674, 2024) of optical-microscopy digital image correlation [OM-DIC] employs high numerical aperture [NA] objectives despite their limited depth of fields, by fending off continual defocusing via automated working distance maintenance. Combining this OM-DIC variant that maximizes optical resolution with robust area scanning, field coverage is expanded to the millimeter scale, capturing deformation of thousands of grains in the region of interest. In this study grain maps are also produced to enable a grain-resolved study of deformation fields; the orientations of each grain are further assigned by electron backscatter diffraction conducted prior to the OM-DIC experiment. An FCC pure Nickel polycrystal specimen is elected with an average of 25 μm grain size. 40x microscopy with the high-NA (=0.42) objective yields on the order of 10^3 DIC points per grain. During the uniaxial load application up to 5% tensile strain, in-situ OM-DIC data is collected at three steps (1.65%, 3.34% and 5%, respectively) to investigate the evolution of intra-grain and inter-grain plastic deformation, as well as interactions between neighboring grains. Accurate grain mapping enables precise segmentation of the grain boundaries, facilitating the extraction of deformation and rotation signals for each individual grain, distinguishing grain cores and grain mantles (the band around the boundary of a grain with each of its neighbors). Given this framework, the objectives of this study are twofold: (i) to derive statistical correlations between mantle and core deformation/rotation of individual grains as a function of crystallographic orientation, and (ii) to derive statistical correlations between sibling mantles (that share the same grain boundary but located in different grains).

Keywords optical microscopy · DIC · polycrystal · high resolution · grain-resolved · grain boundary deformation

Introduction

Digital image correlation has become a prominent strain field measurement technique for both industrial and academic uses. Despite the limited resolution compared to electron microscopy, academic applications [1–4] of DIC combined with optical microscopy provide a measurement capability across different length-scales. These applications are expanding the knowledge of deformation heterogeneity of metallic materials while providing measurement data for calibration of high-fidelity plasticity models [5, 6]. Current applications of OM-DIC have been advancing accuracy and resolution limits by implementing a novel methodology that uses high numerical aperture optics combined with robust area scanning for immense statistics [1–3] and, most recently, extracts strain fields over every individual grain by generating grain masks [7, 8]

Classifying deformation fields into type-I (macroscopic/aggregate average), type-II (intergranular, $\bar{\varepsilon}$), and type-III (intragranular, ε), an OM-DIC setup that can capture type-III strains and calculate the rest by averaging requires high magnification and high numerical aperture (NA) optics. However, these optical settings make the implementation prone to defocusing due to the associated limited depth of field (on the order of a few μm) and are prone to limited field coverage that results from

Olcay Türkoğlu (✉)
Department of Mechanical Engineering Işık University, Sile, Istanbul, 34980, Türkiye
*Corresponding author. e-mail: olcay.turkoglu@isikun.edu.tr

C. Can Aydıner
Department of Mechanical Engineering Boğaziçi University, Bebek, Istanbul, 34342, Türkiye
e-mail: can.aydiner@bogazici.edu.tr

Chi-Hung Hwang et al. (eds.), *Advancement of Optical Methods & Digital Image Correlation in Experimental Mechanics, Vol. 2*, Conference Proceedings
of the Society for Experimental Mechanics Series, https://doi.org/10.13052/9788743808282-2

increased magnification [9]. To address these limitations, this in-house-built OM-DIC setup [1, 2, 7, 8] incorporates an automated working distance maintenance algorithm for precise focusing and a robust area scanning implementation to extend the coverage to millimeter scales. As a result, an average-sized grain in the current study contains on the order of 10^3 subsets (grain-resolved, type-III signals). With full field coverage extended to millimeters, thousands of such grains are sampled, making type-II strains (strains averaged over the domain of each grain) statistically meaningful as well. Furthermore, the high resolution enables averaging over any chosen material subset, e.g, the individual boundary among neighboring grains. While the intragrain data resolution (grain-resolved resolutions) are generally produced with scanning electron microscopy [SEM]-DIC [10, 11] with at times two order higher resolution, the current OM-DIC variant strives to offer meaningful data for polycrystal physics with its higher practicality (leading to abundant in situ data at multiple load points) and high granular statistics.

Here, an FCC pure Nickel polycrystal sample is evaluated due to its simple deformation mechanism and is less likely to exhibit twinning because of relatively high stacking fault energy (90mJ/m^2 [12]). Although deformation of the highest-symmetry FCC metals is considered homogenous in the macro-scale, deformation on the microscale is complex and heterogeneous. Recent studies [5, 6] show that even the elastic deformation of pure Nickel polycrystals is heterogeneous at the intragranular scale. It is commonly postulated [13, 14] that one of the sources of this deformation heterogeneity is accumulation of deformation at the triple-point regions and boundary regions. However, these strain accumulations and difference between grain-boundary and grain-core region deformation are reported for only a few grains in the polycrystalline aggregates [13, 14]. On the other hand, these strain accumulations are observed in different sizes of boundary segments within grains (in order of nanometers to few micrometers). The best of the authors' knowledge, a methodology that statistically investigates core and boundary deformation over relatively large material field is missing. This study aims to lay out certain features of such a methodology with a particular focus on deformation differences over grain-boundary regions (mantle) and core regions in a statistical manner.

Experimental

Commercially pure (99.5%) face-centered-cubic [FCC] Nickel rod (extruded) with 6.25 mm diameter is procured from Alfa-Aesar (Thermo Fisher). The rod was subjected to annealing heat treatment (4 hours at 800° C) and is fully recrystallized, and grain-growth is established (final average grain size: 25 μm). The dog-bone specimen (8 mm gage length and 3x3 mm^2 gage cross section) was precisely machined using wire electric discharge machining [WEDM]. The longitudinal (loading) direction of the tensile specimen was aligned with the extrusion direction of the rod. During the metallography, gradual grinding and extensive polishing with colloidal silica (5nm-particle-size) was applied carefully with automatic grinding machine (QATM Saphire 530). Subsequently, the specimen was minimally etched with diluted Marble's reagent to reveal boundaries without topographic distortions on the grains' surfaces. Prior to the tensile test, specimen was subjected to electron backscattering diffraction [EBSD] and crystallographic orientations of individual grains in the region of interest [ROI] were gathered via AMATEK EDAX detector in a FEI Quanta 400 FEG SEM.

The custom DIC setup depicted in Figure 1 (a) comprises several key components. First, there are the stationary optical lines, which include a macroscopic line—featuring a FLIR Grasshopper 3 camera with a 2.3 MP Sony IMX174 monochrome sensor and an Edmund Optics 0.5x telecentric lens—and a microscopic line, which uses another FLIR Grasshopper 3 camera equipped with a 5 MP Sony IMX250 monochrome sensor, a Navitar Ultrazoom 6000 tube lens, and a high-NA (=0.42) Mitutoyo M Plan APO 20x objective with a 0.1 μm/pixel field length. Second, the setup includes a small form factor tension-compression load frame (10 kN, Kammrath & Weiss). Third, an X-Y-Z positioning array (Newport M-ILS series for X-Y and GTS30V for the vertical Z positioner) is employed. The entire system is mounted on a Newport RS4000 vibration isolation table, and in-house instrument software automates the coordination of both the cameras and the stage motions.

Continuous strain monitoring is conducted under the macroscopic line using live macro-DIC analysis during the tensile test. At selected load steps shown in Figure 1 (b), the sample is transferred beneath the micro-DIC line, where micro-DIC area scans (X-Y) capture the images of the surface over a predefined grid of overlapping frames. These overlaps facilitate the seamless merging of both image and data fields (e.g., strain). In this experiment, the frame matrix consists of 13$\times$7 images covering an overall ROI of approximately 2$\times$0.8 mm^2. (Images of this domain and further details of sample and setup are provided elsewhere [8]; a study that uses different data from the same experiment to explore elastics strain upon unloads and the possibility to evaluate stresses.)

DIC analysis is performed using a Gauss-Newton inverse composition algorithm with 61$\times$61 pixel subsets (6$\times$6 μm^2) and 10 pixels (1 μm) grid spacing. The gradient of the displacement then calculated by using 3$\times$3 Savitzky-Golay differentiation kernel to determine local strains [15].

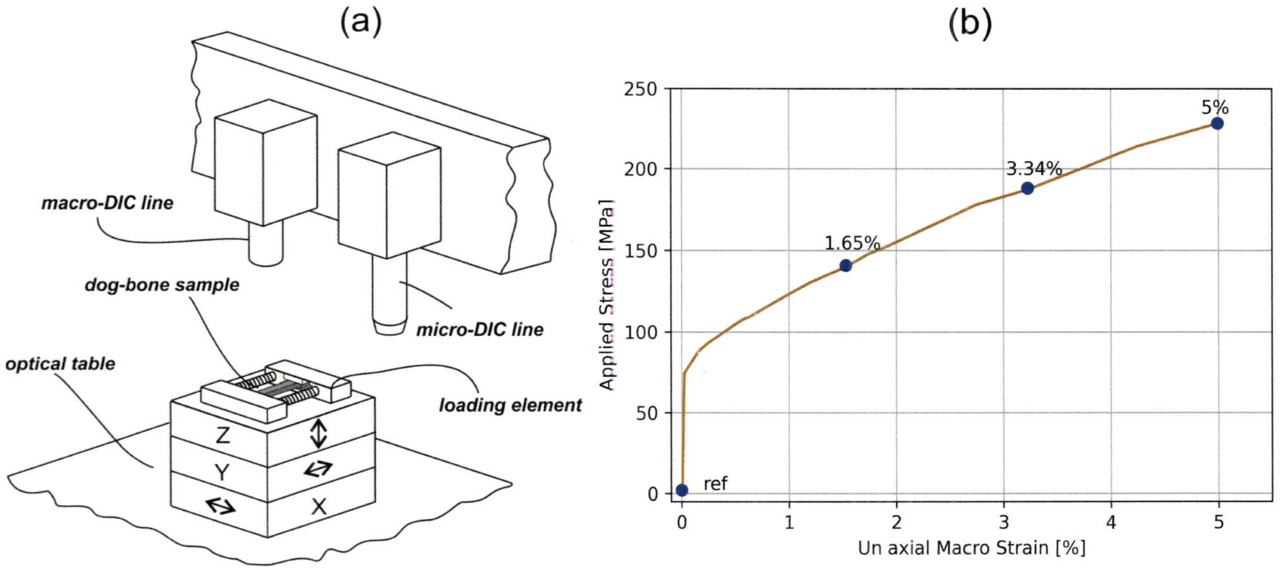

Fig. 1 (a) Experimental setup, (b) Macro tensile curve

Before the in-situ micro-DIC experiment and speckle pattern application (but after metallography to reveal grain boundaries), a complete area-scan is conducted to image the full ROI. Avoiding the concealing effect of the speckles on grain boundaries, an accurate grain mask (boundary map) that enables the extraction of grain-resolved information is manually generated over this image, using precise Bezier curves. The grain mask is then compared/verified with the grains identified in the EBSD analysis, and the crystallographic orientations are registered for each identified grain. Approximately 3000 grains are identified/indexed with their exact morphology (grain mask) and crystallographic orientation. Subsequently, the speckle pattern is applied using a unique method prior to the reference DIC scan. Finally, the grain mask undergoes a precise affine transformation to correct for small tilts and distortions introduced during the demounting and remounting of the tensile specimen, before and after the speckle pattern application (see [8] for details of the grain mask extraction procedure). As a result, the image fields of the reference load point and the utilized grain mask are exactly aligned. The micro-DIC experiment is conducted in-situ, with micro-DIC conducted at multiple loading points as the tensile load is advanced in position control. Figure 1 (b) shows the three field-average strain levels up to 5% where results are presented in this paper.

The defining trait of postprocessing in this type of study is to explore strains per grain, and over other polycrystal morphological features, e.g., material bands about grain boundaries. For this, after the experiment and DIC analyses are conducted, strain signal of each grain is processed with morphological operations. First, strains over grain boundaries are discounted, using a binary erosion algorithm over the grain mask. [Although a DIC speckle pattern should be random and isotropic, continuous lines of the grain boundaries in OM images compromise these aspects. As a result, a possible source of DIC error is eliminated. The data over grain boundaries do not belong to any individual grain anyways.] Secondly, after this initial peeling of the outer layer of the grain (discounting red zones in Figure 2), more layers (n, up to 5) are removed, as schematically shown in the light grey lines for n=2 in Figure 2. The region of each grain around its core that is bounded by the gray (n=2, two-layer-stripped) boundaries will be referred to as the grain core in the rest of the text. However, the boundary obviously loops through multiple neighboring grains (a total of 7 neighbors for the central grain in Figure 2) and we propose to investigate each boundary segment independently. To this end, another morphological algorithm slices the overall boundary region with lines that connect the centroids [CM] of each grain and triple points. An imaginary triangular slice of the relevant grain is extracted via a CM and triple points (refer to dashed grey lines in Figure 2); then, an inward binary dilation algorithm is applied to the boundary segment of this slice multiple times (n, up to 5). As a result, bands of material inside a grain that is closest to each neighboring grain are distinguished. As such one can extract the strains of the central grain in the vicinity of its boundary with neighbor 1. This region is called the mantle 0-1 on Figure 2; indicating the band region inside grain 0 but neighboring grain 1. The opposite mantle region inside grain 1 is analogously called mantle 1-0.

The CM-to-triple-point bisection prevents the repetitive use of subsets near the boundary region, ensuring that the average strain for each mantle (0-1, 0-2, etc.) is computed from non-overlapping data. After generating masks for both the core and mantle regions of the grains, the DIC strain signals inside each grain (type-III) are locally averaged over both regions. The result of this operation is shown in Figure 2 for axial strains with a colormap.

Results and Discussion

Local results from the exemplified neighborhood

Following the average strain extraction method described in the previous section, a sample neighborhood is selected within the overall ROI [8], as indicated in Figure 2. At the center of this neighborhood, an average-sized grain (grain 0) is highlighted, with its mantle and core regions depicted in colors corresponding to their respective average axial strain values at 5% macroscopic strain. While the average axial core strains of some neighboring grains (n3, n4) are comparable to the applied macroscopic strain, others (n1, n5, n6) exhibit larger strain values. Considering that the neighborhood is relatively small (approximately $40 \times 40 \mu\,\mathrm{m}^2$), these variations in average axial strain across local regions (which can be deemed type-II strains) are significant (numerical values are provided in Table 1).

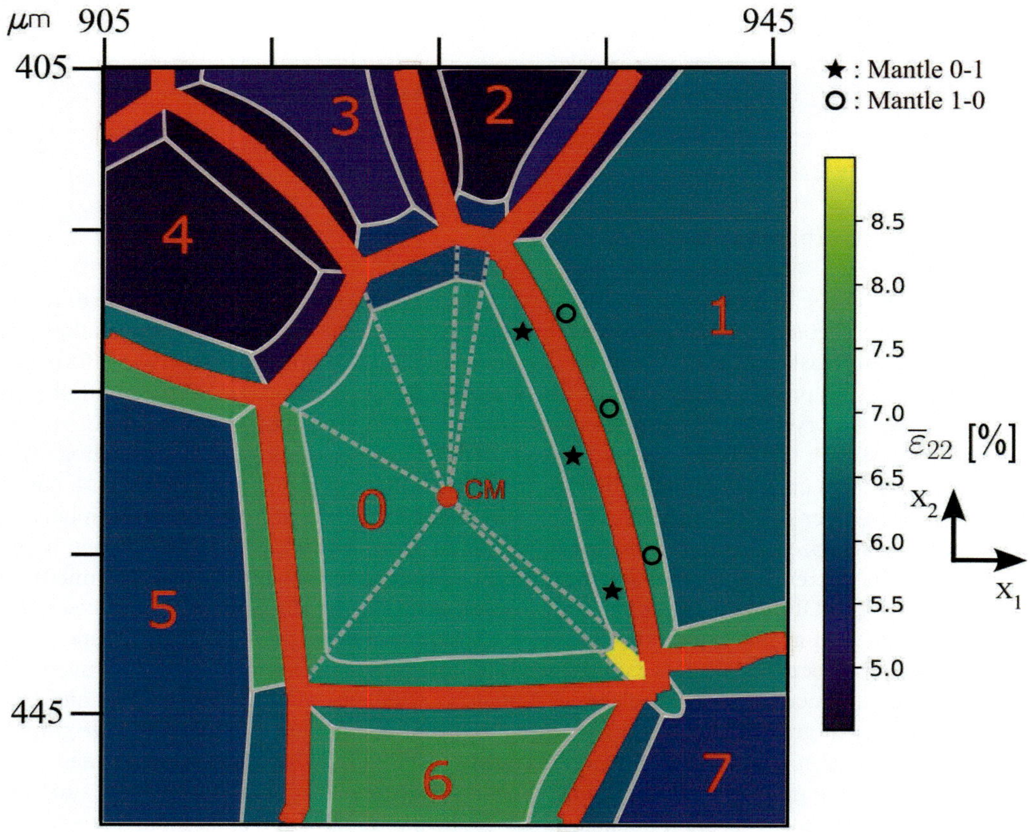

Fig. 2 Mantle-averaged and core-averaged strains of the selected grain and neighboring grain cores and mantles (n=2)

Table 1 presents the average strain values for both the axial and transverse directions for the sample neighborhood. The column headers indicate the neighboring grain numbers, while the row headers list E_{hkl} (directional stiffness along tensile direction), in-grain mantle strains (e.g. Mantle 0-1, Mantle 0-2, etc.), in-neighbor mantle strains (e.g. Mantle 1-0, Mantle 2-0, etc.) and core strains of neighboring grains. The mantles 0-2 and 0-7 are, however, too small to draw conclusions from and the corresponding rows in Table 1 are shaded gray. In case of $\overline{\varepsilon}_{11}$, the average mantle strains within the center grain vary from –0.7% to –2.8%, indicating a higher degree of dispersion in transverse strains compared to the axial strain, $\overline{\varepsilon}_{22}$. Interestingly, even among neighboring mantles(e.g., Mantle 0-1 and Mantle 1-0), the average transverse strains can differ significantly (–1.3% vs. –4.7%), which is consistent with the large differences in transverse strains among the core strains in the neighborhood (core 0: –1.7%; core 1: –4.0%). Axial strain, in contrast, are quite more regulated. Similar observations have been made for elastic strains (upon unload) [8].

Additionally, the directional stiffness—calculated based on crystallographic orientation ascertained by prior EBSD—of neighboring grains may be an important effective factor behind the observed deformation heterogeneity. For example, the center grain exhibits relatively high directional stiffness, while grain n1 has the lowest and n6 has a stiffness similar to that of the center grain. However, the axial and transverse strain averages in these neighborhoods (0-1 and 0-6) do not show a direct correlation between directional stiffness and the average strains accumulated over the boundaries or core regions at 5%, i.e., significant plastic strain. The data is analyzed with a statistically sufficient number of grains for this and similar correlations currently and the findings will be shared elsewhere in the future. Some aspects of the strain variation across the full-field (entire ROI) that focuses on core-mantle variations is presented in the next section.

Table 1 Mantle-averaged and core-averaged strains of the selected grain and neighboring grain cores and mantles

	n1	n2	n3	n4	n5	n6	n7
E_{hkl} [GPa] (Center Grain: 302GPa)	148	297	159	227	164	302	265
Mantle Strain ($\bar{\varepsilon}_{22}$) (in-grain) [%]	6.9	6.0	6.0	6.9	7.6	7.0	9.8
Mantle Strain ($\bar{\varepsilon}_{22}$) (in-neighbor) [%]	7.2	5.8	5.7	5.0	7.6	6.8	6.8
Core Strain ($\bar{\varepsilon}_{22}$) [%] (Center Grain: 7%)	6.4	4.5	5.0	4.3	5.8	7.6	5.6
Mantle Strain ($\bar{\varepsilon}_{11}$) (in-grain) [%]	-1.3	-0.1	-0.7	-1	-2.8	-2	-5
Mantle Strain ($\bar{\varepsilon}_{11}$) (in-neighbor) [%]	-4.7	0.3	-0.7	-1.2	0	-2.7	-4.4
Core Strain ($\bar{\varepsilon}_{11}$) [%] (Center Grain: -1.7%)	-4.0	-0.8	-1.5	-1.6	-1.2	-3	-2.4

Statistical (full-field) results

Statistical results for all mantles/cores (as defined in the sample domain of Figure 1) are drawn from the entire ROI as long as the grains meet the following criteria for strain/orientation data health: (i) grain size should be larger than 12μ m, ensuring that at least approximately 100 subsets are available in the grain-resolved domain, (ii) grains are not located in the stitching region among individual frames of the area-scan [8], and (iii) grains have a high EBSD confidence index ($CI > 0.65$). After this filtering, a total of 1290 grains are obtained, comprising 7823 mantles overall.

From a statistical point of view, first, average strain distributions of mantle and core regions are investigated at each load point. However, histograms are not used to present these distributions because the total number of core regions and mantle regions are not equal (which yields much more different frequencies on the y-axis of regular histograms, comparing histograms becomes difficult). Instead of histograms, Weibull probability density functions are fitted to all strain distributions and these are presented. Unlike the more typical Gaussian distributions, Weibull distributions allow asymmetrical distributions and provide statistically better fits for surface strain components, $\bar{\varepsilon}_{11}$, $\bar{\varepsilon}_{22}$ and $\bar{\varepsilon}_{12}$. Therefore, the following figures in this are represented as Weibull distribution with probability densities. The minimum r^2 value in the fits is calculated as 0.97 that justifies the use of Weibull fits to the data in this presentation .

In Figure 3 (a-c), surface strain components $\bar{\varepsilon}_{11}$, $\bar{\varepsilon}_{22}$ and $\bar{\varepsilon}_{12}$ are presented, respectively. Each part, contains results for all load points (macroscopic strains 1.65, 3.34 and 5%) to present the evolution of the distributions. The results are distinguished over the core (solid lines) and mantle (dashed lines) regions. As a result, the first apparent conclusion that can be drawn from these distributions is that the mantle distributions exhibit a higher strain range. Moreover, as macroscopic strain increases, the strain range in the mantles tends to increase, along with increase in strain heterogeneity between grains. The reduction in probability density combined with the increase in strain range after the load increment clearly demonstrates this behavior. While most reports in the literature indicate that mantles (more precisely, grain boundary segments) accumulate high strains [3, 9, 10], the distributions in Figure 3 (a–c) reveal that some mantle regions exhibit smaller strains than the core, even though most mantles show strain levels similar to those of the cores. Note $\bar{\varepsilon}_{12}$ median values are approximately equal to zero in this uniaxial loading, which can be considered as a sanity check. Similarly, the median/mean ratios of normal strains ($-\bar{\varepsilon}_{11}/\bar{\varepsilon}_{22}$, Poisson's ratio) yields the expected 0.5. Over a full statistical average (also equivalent to averaging of the shown distributions), strains in the mantle regions are similar to those in the core regions, i.e., there is no apparent higher strain in the mantles.

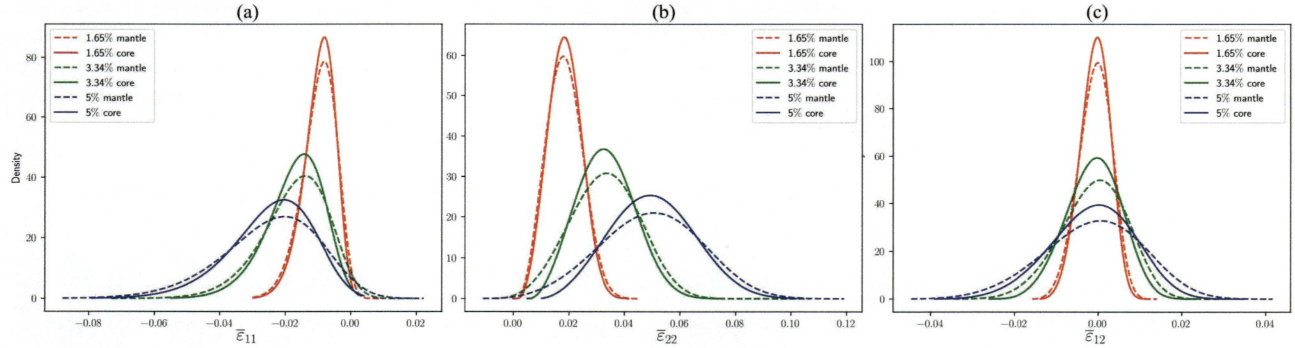

Fig. 3 Strain distribution evolution of core and mantle strains (a) $\overline{\varepsilon}_{11}$, (b) $\overline{\varepsilon}_{22}$ and (c) $\overline{\varepsilon}_{12}$

A more compound metric is considered next in Figure 4, delineating the local difference between mantle and core strains. For this, the average strains of each mantle are normalized by the average strain at the core of the particular grain. Figure 4 (a-c) shows these normalized strain distributions. As a general result, median values of these strain ratios are approximately equal to one, supporting the notion that the highest fraction of mantles and cores have similar strains in this polycrystalline aggregate. Core-normalized $\overline{\varepsilon}_{22}$ ($\overline{\varepsilon}_{22\ mantle}/\ \overline{\varepsilon}_{22\ core}$) distributions (Figure 4 (b)) seem more regularized than other strain components which are expected due to their alignment with the tensile direction. While macroscopic strain increases, core-normalized $\overline{\varepsilon}_{22}$ distributions show a tendency to spread. In particular, when 1.65% and 3.34% macroscopic strains are compared, range of core-normalized $\overline{\varepsilon}_{22}$ increases significantly. However, when the macroscopic strain increased from 3.34% to 5%, the increase in the range of core-normalized $\overline{\varepsilon}_{22}$ is limited. A similar behavior is also observed for core-normalized $\overline{\varepsilon}_{11}$ and $\overline{\varepsilon}_{12}$ (Figure 4 (a), (c)), however the range of strain ratios differs significantly as well as probability densities. Since the nominal value of $\overline{\varepsilon}_{12}$=0, large values tend to occur with both positive and negative senses in Figure 4 (c), which should not be assigned a physical significance. Core-normalized $\overline{\varepsilon}_{11}$ shows a larger spread than core-normalized $\overline{\varepsilon}_{22}$, in line with the previous observations.

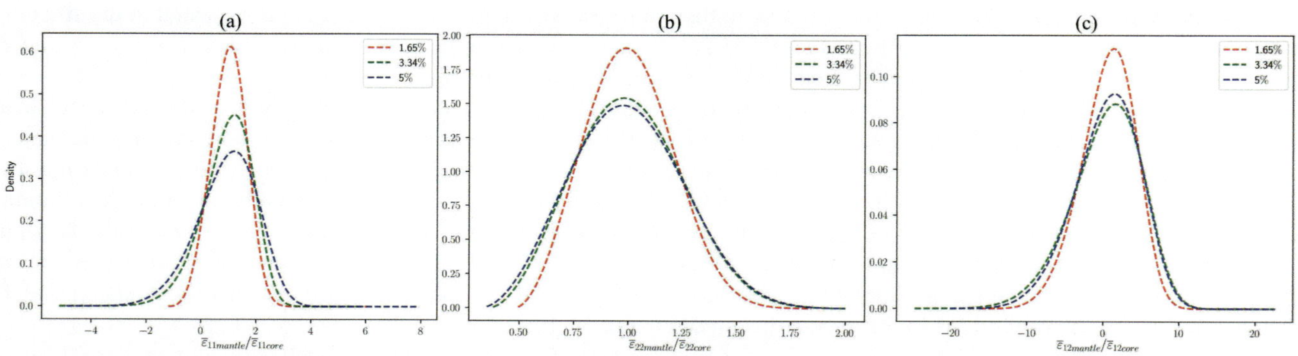

Fig. 4 Strain ratio of mantle and core strains at 5% macroscopic strain, (a) $\overline{\varepsilon}_{11\ mantle}/\ \overline{\varepsilon}_{11\ core}$, (b) $\overline{\varepsilon}_{22\ mantle}/\ \overline{\varepsilon}_{22\ core}$ and (c)

The mantle thickness in the above evaluations have been taken as two data layers of grains (each layer approximately 1 μm thick). Figure 5 (a-c) studies the dependence of the shown results on the assumed mantle band thickness. Thicknesses up to 6 data layers (6 μm) are considered and the average strain response of the mantles are shown. Although, 5% macroscopic load point which shows the most dispersive average strain behavior for mantles is selected, the variance of the Weibull distributions of different mantle thickness still shows a very similar behavior and no significant difference is observed in both ranges and probability densities. (Note that one-layer-thick mantles are not included in computations to increase numbers of the subsets in the averaging zone.) Consequently, the distributions shown are robust against mantle thickness variations.

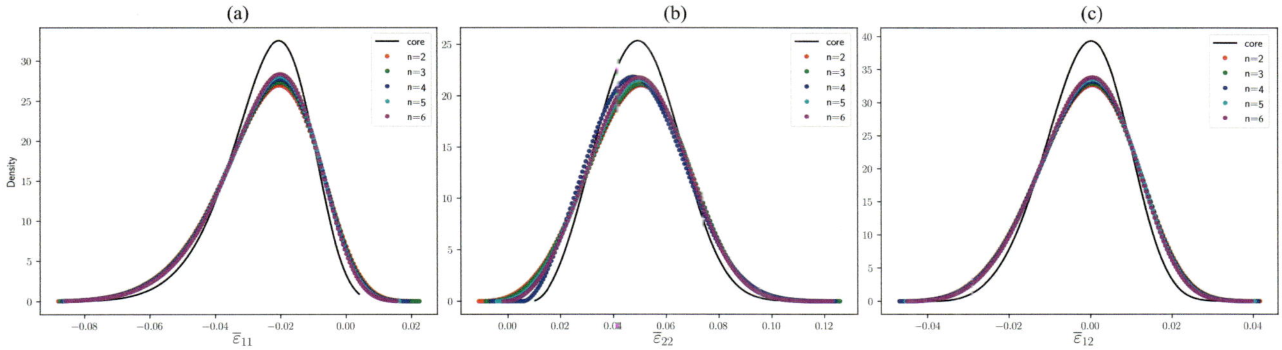

Fig. 5 Strain distribution response of varying mantle band widths (n=2,..,6 roughly corresponds to n=2,..,6 μm) at 5% macroscopic strain (a) $\overline{\varepsilon}_{11}$, (b) $\overline{\varepsilon}_{22}$ and (c) $\overline{\varepsilon}_{12}$

Conclusion

To conclude, this OM-DIC variant, which employs high numerical aperture and high magnification optics, provides a field resolution comparable to that achieved in coarse SEM-DIC applications, thereby enabling grain-resolved deformation research. Furthermore, robust area scanning expands the coverage to millimeter scales while capturing deformation signals for thousands of grains. This preliminary study offers a prospective framework that demonstrates differences in strains between the core and mantle regions of individual grains in a polycrystalline aggregate. As shown in the exemplified results, even though the analyzed neighborhood is relatively small (approximately $40 \times 40 \mu \text{ m}^2$), significant deformation heterogeneity is observed both within individual grains and across the local neighborhood. The full-field results contain deformation statistics that compare core and mantle regions. In future work, these statistics will be further investigated by considering factors such as directional stiffness, Schmidt factors, grain-resolved rotation, and variations in core and mantle sizes, thereby advancing our understanding of deformation heterogeneity and facilitating experimental comparisons with high-fidelity plasticity models.

Acknowledgments O.T. acknowledges the financial support of the Scientific and Technological Research Council of Turkey (TÜBİTAK) through the 2224-A Grant Program and Işık University, which enabled travel and participation in the 2025 SEM Annual Conference.

References

1. Shafaghi N, Kapan E, Aydıner CC, Cyclic Strain Heterogeneity and Damage Formation in Rolled Magnesium Via In Situ Microscopic Image Correlation, Exp Mech, 60:735–751, 2020, https://doi.org/10.1007/s11340-020-00612-6
2. Özdür NA, Üçel IB, Yang J, Aydıner CC, Residual Intensity as a Morphological Identifier of Twinning Fields in Microscopic Image Correlation, Exp Mech, 2020 https://doi.org/10.1007/s11340-020-00672-8
3. Aydıner CC, Telemez MA Multiscale deformation heterogeneity in twinning magnesium investigated with in situ image correlation, Int J Plast 56:203–218, 2014 https://doi.org/10.1016/j.ijplas.2013.12.001
4. Carroll, J., W. Abuzaid, J. Lambros and H. Sehitoglu, "An Experimental Methodology to Relate Local Strain to Microstructural Texture", Review of Scientific Instruments, Vol. 81, No. 8, p. 83703, 2010, https://doi.org/10.1063/1.3474902
5. P. Eisenlohr, M. Diehl, R.A. Lebensohn, F. Roters, A spectral method solution to crystal elasto-viscoplasticity at finite strains, Int J Plast, 46:37-53, 2013. https://doi.org/10.1016/j.ijplas.2012.09.012
6. Jiahao Cheng, Jinlei Shen, Raj K. Mishra, Somnath Ghosh, Discrete twin evolution in Mg alloys using a novel crystal plasticity finite element model, Acta Mater, 149:142-153, 2018, https://doi.org/10.1016/j.actamat.2018.02.032
7. Türkoğlu, O. and C. C. Aydıner, "Enabling Digital Image Correlation with High Resolution Microscopic Optics via Working Distance Automation: Advancing Resolution and Accuracy Limits", SEM2022: Advancements in Optical Methods, Digital Image Correlation & Micro-and Nanomechanics, Vol. 4, pp. 49–56, Springer International Publishing, Cham, 2023, https://doi.org/10.1007/978-3-031-17471-1_9
8. Türkoğlu, O., Aydıner, C. An Exploration of Grain-Averaged Stress Measurement Using Partial Unloads with In situ Microscopic Image Correlation, Exp Mech 64:655–674, 2024. https://doi.org/10.1007/s11340-024-01050-4
9. Padilla HA, Lambros J, Beaudoin AJ, Robertson IM, Relating inhomogeneous deformation to local texture in zirconium through grain-scale digital image correlation strain mapping experiments. Int J Solids Struct, 49:18–31, 2012, https://doi.org/10.1016/j.ijsolstr.2011.09.001
10. J.C. Stinville, N. Vanderesse, F. Bridier, P. Bocher, T.M. Pollock, High resolution mapping of strain localization near twin boundaries in a nickel-based superalloy, Acta Mater, 98:29-42, 2015 https://doi.org/10.1016/j.actamat.2015.07.016.

11. Kammers, A.D., Daly, S. Self-Assembled Nanoparticle Surface Patterning for Improved Digital Image Correlation in a Scanning Electron Microscope. Exp Mech, 53:1333–1341, 2013. https://doi.org/10.1007/s11340-013-9734-5
12. Hertzberg, R. W., Deformation and Fracture Mechanics of Engineering Materials,4th edn., J. Wiley & Sons, New York, 1996.
13. H.-H. Fu, D.J. Benson, M.A. Meyers, Analytical and computational description of effect of grain size on yield stress of metals, Acta Mater, 49-13: 2567-2582 2001, https://doi.org/10.1016/S1359-6454(01)00062-3
14. Wael Z. Abuzaid, Michael D. Sangid, Jay D. Carroll, Huseyin Sehitoglu, John Lambros, Slip transfer and plastic strain accumulation across grain boundaries in Hastelloy X, J. Mech. Phys. Solids. 60-6:1201-1220, 2012, https://doi.org/10.1016/j.jmps.2012.02.001
15. Pan, B., K. Li and W. Tong, Fast, Robust and Accurate Digital Image Correlation Calculation Without Redundant Computations, Exp Mech, 53:1277–1289, 2013, https://doi.org/10.1007/s11340-013-9717-6

Chapter 3
Residual Stress Evaluation in Silicon Wafer Based on the Principle of Superposition and Full-Field Warpage Measurement

Satoru Yoneyama, Keisuke Iizuka, and Mitsuaki Kudo

Abstract A method for estimating residual stresses in silicon wafers from optically measured full-field warpage is proposed. The warpage of a silicon wafer is measured with a surface profilometer equipped with a laser displacement meter. To establish the relationship between warpage and residual stresses, a finite element method is used to calculate the warpage distribution for unit positive stress on the front surface and unit negative stress on the back surface, applied to a single pair of front and back elements. This process is repeated for all such pairs, yielding numerous sets of relationships between warpage and unit initial stresses. Based on the principle of superposition, the measured warpage is expressed as a combination of these unit initial stress-induced warpages. The warpage distribution is then obtained through a least-squares method, with regularization applied to derive appropriate residual stress values. The proposed method is applied to measured warpage distributions of actual silicon wafers, successfully yielding residual stress estimations. The results demonstrate the effectiveness of the proposed method for evaluating residual stresses in silicon wafers.

Keywords Optical method · Residual stress · Silicon wafer · Warpage · Principle of superposition

Introduction

In the manufacturing process of silicon wafers, residual stresses are induced due to the temperature gradients in the wafer and the influence of the surface processing layer generated during grinding. Such residual stresses cause warpage and peeling, which induce defects in products. An X-ray diffraction method or a hole-drilling method is generally used for measuring residual stresses in metallic materials. However, an X-ray diffraction method is usually difficult to measure the residual stresses in single crystals such as silicon. Efforts have been made to measure the residual stresses in silicon single crystals using an X-ray diffraction method, but such special techniques have not yet been generalized. A hole-drilling method is destructive and not suitable for inspecting silicon wafers.

Methods for measuring residual stress in silicon wafers have been studied because of their importance and difficulty. Then, various techniques for evaluating the residual stresses in silicon wafers including simulation have been reported [1]. On the other hand, in the quality inspection of silicon wafers, the warpage is often measured using an interferometer or a laser displacement meter [2]. Therefore, it would be very convenient if the residual stresses in the silicon wafers could be evaluated from the warpage distribution. By achieving this, it is expected that the manufacturing process will be improved based on the evaluation results of residual stresses. In addition, it is important to know the residual stresses in the silicon wafers because they are an important index for predicting the device life. Toyama et al. [3] proposed a method for evaluating stresses inducing the warpage of silicon wafer from warpage measurement. However, they estimated not the residual stresses themselves but the stresses causing the warpage. Obata et al. [4] proposed a method for evaluating residual stresses in a silicon wafer from full field warpage measurement. In their method, the residual stresses are estimated using the regularized least-squares method based on the principle of superposition.

In this study, a method for estimating residual stresses in silicon wafers from optically measured full-field warpage is proposed by improving the previously proposed method. The proposed method is applied to the measured warpage distributions

Satoru Yoneyama · Keisuke Iizuka · Mitsuaki Kudo
Department of Mechanical EngineeringAoyama Gakuin University, Sagamihara 252-5258, Japan
e-mail: yoneyama@me.aoyama.ac.jp; iizuka@me.aoyama.ac.jp; c5624144@aoyama.jp

Chi-Hung Hwang et al. (eds.), *Advancement of Optical Methods & Digital Image Correlation in Experimental Mechanics, Vol. 2*, Conference Proceedings
of the Society for Experimental Mechanics Series, https://doi.org/10.13052/9788743808282-3

of actual silicon wafers, successfully yielding residual stress estimations. The results demonstrate the effectiveness of the proposed method for evaluating residual stresses in silicon wafers.

Method

The warpage of a 200-mm diameter, 725-micrometer thick silicon wafer is measured with a surface profilometer equipped with a laser displacement meter, providing a measurement resolution of 10 nanometers and a spatial resolution of 1 micrometer. It is assumed that the warpage is caused by residual stresses, with those on the front surface in equilibrium with those on the back. To establish the relationship between warpage and residual stresses, a finite element method is used to calculate the warpage distribution for unit positive stress on the front surface and unit negative stress on the back surface, applied to a single pair of front and back elements. This process is repeated for all such pairs, yielding numerous sets of relationships between warpage and unit initial stresses. Based on the principle of superposition, the measured warpage is expressed as a combination of these unit initial stress-induced warpages. The warpage distribution is then obtained through a least-squares method, with regularization applied to derive appropriate residual stress values.

Results

Figure 1 shows the warpage distribution of a 200-mm diameter, 725-micrometer thick silicon wafer obtained using a surface profilometer. By applying the proposed method, the warpage distribution is obtained from the many sets of the finite element results using the least-squares method, as shown in Fig. 2. The residual between the measured warpage in Fig. 1 and the estimated warpage is 2.72×10^{-2} μm, indicating the measured warpage can be approximated based on the principle of superposition.

The residual stresses are also obtained based on the principle of superposition. However, the coefficients obtained using a least-squares method cannot guarantee the uniqueness of the solution. That is, there exists multiple solutions for a single warpage distribution. Figure 3 shows the residual stress distributions obtained using an ordinary least-squares method. It is observed that the high stress values are obtained, and the distributions are unnatural. The inappropriate variation of the stresses in Fig. 3 indicate the regularization scheme should be introduced into the last-squares method.

The residual stresses obtained using the regularized least squares method are shown in Fig. 4. It can be seen that smooth and appropriate values of stresses are obtained.

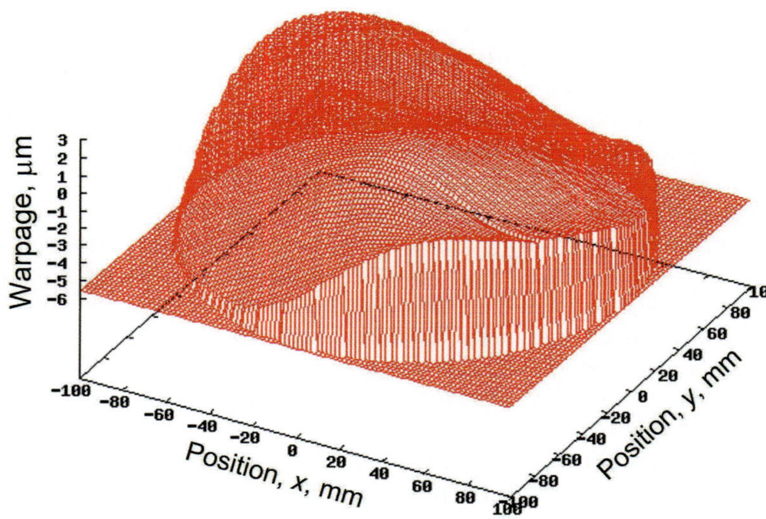

Fig. 1 Warpage distribution of the silicon wafer measured using a surface profilometer equipped with a laser displacement meter

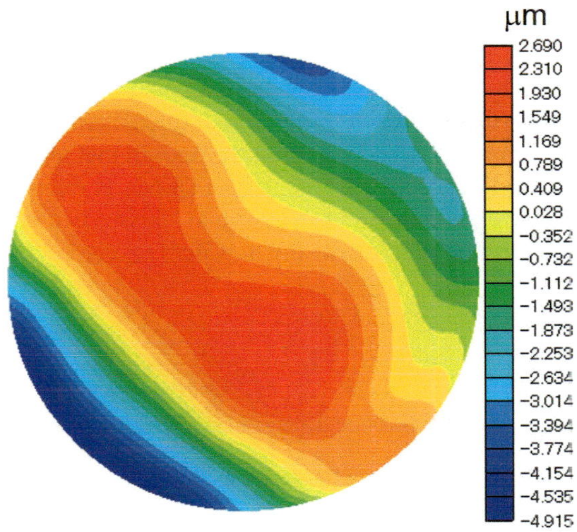

Fig. 2 Contour map of the warpage distribution of the silicon wafer obtained using the least-squares method based on the principle of superposition

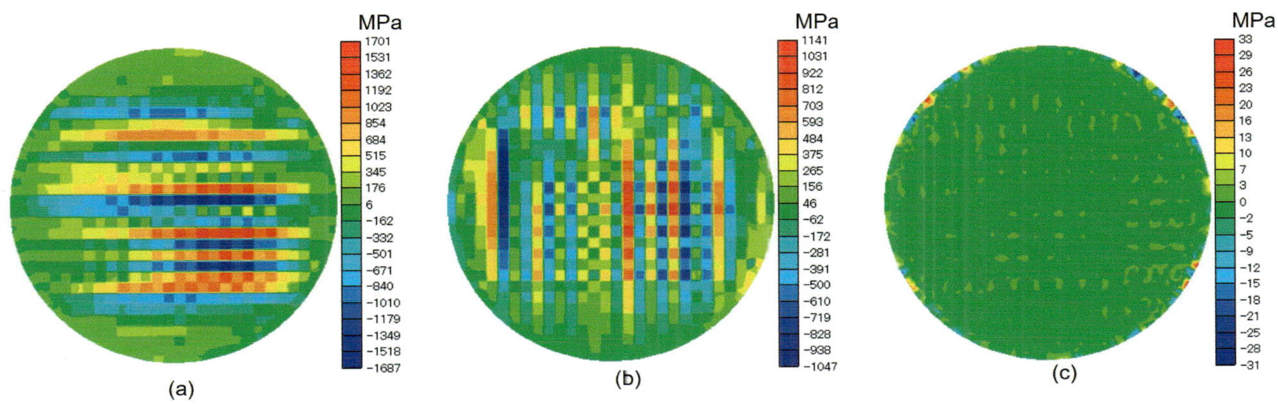

Fig. 3 Residual stresses estimated using the ordinary least-squares method: (a) σ_x; (b)σ_y; (c)τ_{xy}

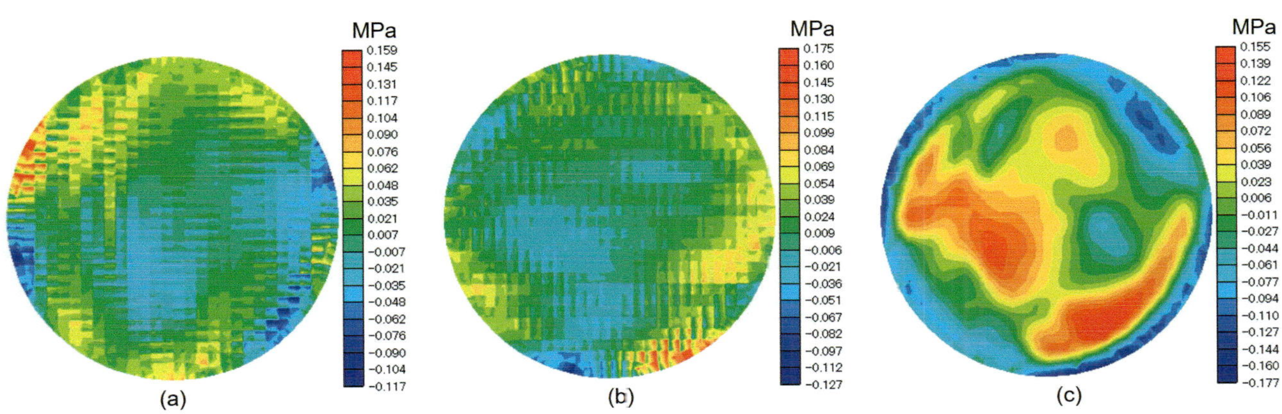

Fig. 4 Residual stresses estimated using the regularized least-squares method: (a) σ_x; (b)σ_y; (c)σ_{xy}

Conclusions

This paper proposes a method for estimating the residual stresses in a silicon wafer from the warpage measurement. The warpage of a finite element model is determined from the measured values using a least-squares method. The residual stresses induced simultaneously with the warpage are estimated. The proposed method is successfully applied to the residual stress evaluation of an actual silicon wafer. Because the warpage of a silicon is often measured in the inspection process, the proposed method which uses the warpage for estimating the residual stresses is useful. Therefore, it is expected that the proposed method can be applied to the inspection process of silicon wafers.

References

1. Takahashi, S., Zhou, L. and Shimizu, J., Evaluation of subsurface damage in silicon wafer bases on deflection analysis (in Japanese), J. Jpn. Soc. Precision Eng., 83, 426–32 (2017).
2. Schajer, G.S., Roy, G., Flaman, M.T. and Lu, J., Hole-drilling and ring core method, Handbook of Measurement of Residual Stresses (Lu, J., ed.), Lilburn, Fairmont Press, 5–34 (1996).
3. Toyama, N., Zhang, Y., Yoneyama,S., Kuwabara, S. and Takano, H., Estimating stresses generated in silicon wafer from measured deflection distribution, Adv. Exp. Mech., 6, 33–38 (2021).
4. Obata, Y., Sekino, K. Takeo, K. and Yoneyama, S., Estimating residual stresses of silicon wafer from Measured full-field deflection distribution, Op. Lasers Eng., 148, 106781 (2022).

Chapter 4
GPU-Accelerated Triangulation in the Stereo-DIC Algorithm Using a Heterogeneous Framework

Mullai Thiagu, Rupesh Nasre, and Sankara J. Subramanian

Abstract Stereo-DIC is a well-established non-contact, optical technique used to measure surface deformation. Recent advancements aim to improve both computation speed and accuracy of the stereo-DIC algorithm, facilitating real-time analysis of stereo image pairs captured during in-situ experiments. Previous studies in literature have demonstrated that leveraging a high-performance parallel computing platform, such as a GPU, can significantly improve computation speed for operations that are data-independent. While there is evidence that GPUs enhance the overall speedup factor, a comprehensive analysis of the implementation of each individual step of the stereo-DIC algorithm is yet to be discussed. The purpose of this work is to efficiently implement the stereo triangulation step using a GPU. It is to be noted that the stereo triangulation step is performed twice to calculate the full-field, surface displacement vectors between two stereo image pairs. In this work, a heterogeneous framework consisting of an Intel Xeon octa-core CPU and a Nvidia Tesla K20C GPU card is deployed. The CPU is used for pre-processing tasks such as transfer of spatial coordinates derived from stereo correlation and camera calibration matrix parameters, whereas the GPU is used to implement the triangulation process. By harnessing parallelism both within a thread block and across multiple thread blocks in a Compute Unified Device Architecture (CUDA) programming model, the triangulation process is executed concurrently. It is observed that when the total number of spatial co-ordinates to be triangulated ranges from 50 to 10,000, the overall speedup factor improves by $\approx 758\times$ to $\approx 232\times$.

Keywords Three-dimensional digital image correlation (3D-DIC) · Stereo triangulation · Camera calibration matrix · Heterogeneous framework · Graphics Processing Unit (GPU)

Introduction

In literature, it is well established that the stereo-DIC algorithm is primarily deployed to measure both in-plane and out-of-plane (i.e. surface) deformations of arbitrarily shaped specimens [2], [3]. A conventional stereo-DIC algorithm encompasses three important steps : a) stereo correlation, b) left/right temporal correlation and c) stereo triangulation. Firstly, the purpose of stereo correlation step is to compute the disparity values of subsets between left and right images captured of a specimen before deformation. On the other hand, the objective of the temporal correlation step is to trace the movement of the subset centroids in the reference (undeformed) stereo image pair along the left/right camera image(s). Here, the in-plane flow of optical vectors for respective subsets is tracked between sequences of left/right camera images captured during the deformation process by using two-dimensional digital image correlation technique. The third step (i.e. stereo triangulation) is carried out individually for reference stereo image pair as well as deformed stereo image pair, to reconstruct the 3D coordinates of point correspondences. Finally, difference between the triangulated reference and triangulated deformed surface(s) is calculated to

Mullai Thiagu
Department of Computer Science, SIAS, Krea University, Sri City - 517 646, Andhra Pradesh, India
e-mail: mullai.thiagu@krea.edu.in

Rupesh Nasre
Department of Computer Science and Engineering, Indian Institute of Technology, Madras, Chennai-600 036, Tamil Nadu, India
e-mail: rupesh@cse.iitm.ac.in

Sankara J. Subramanian
Co-Founder, CTO, PhotoGAUGE
e-mail: shankar.j.subramanian@gmail.com

Chi-Hung Hwang et al. (eds.), *Advancement of Optical Methods & Digital Image Correlation in Experimental Mechanics, Vol. 2*, Conference Proceedings
of the Society for Experimental Mechanics Series, https://doi.org/10 13052/9788743808282-4

yield full-field, surface displacement/strain data. The purpose of this paper is to implement the stereo triangulation computation of the reference and deformed surface using a GPU. This step has the scope for massive data parallelism and therefore the approach elucidated by the authors in their previous works [4], [5] is adopted here as well to study the impact of a heterogeneous (CPU-GPU) framework towards improving the computation speed of the stereo triangulation step. As explained in our earlier works, we refer to the technique in which parallelism is achieved across thread blocks[1] as *inter-parallelism* and parallelism within a thread block as *intra-parallelism*. We propose to use a heterogeneous (CPU-GPU) framework and evaluate the gain in speedup factor on a typical stereo-DIC dataset. The remainder of the paper is organized as follows: in the next section , we discuss the background details of the heterogeneous framework, followed by the analysis of results in Section 3 and concluding remarks in Section 4.

Background

Stereo triangulation is the process of finding the position of an object point in three-dimensional space given its positions in the stereo image pair acquired using the calibrated stereo rig [1]. As illustrated in Figure 1, this process is applied on a group of corresponding camera coordinate object points derived from stereo correlation step applied between the rectified reference stereo image pair ($\mathbf{I}^{\mathbf{RL}_1}, \mathbf{I}^{\mathbf{RR}_1}$). The spatial coordinates of corresponding points (i.e., $\mathbf{X}_1^{\mathbf{L}}, \mathbf{Y}_1^{\mathbf{L}}, \mathbf{X}_1^{\mathbf{R}}, \mathbf{Y}_1^{\mathbf{R}}$) within a stereo image pair in the camera coordinate system are transformed onto a set of distinct 3D object points (i.e., $\mathbf{X}_1^{\mathbf{3D}}, \mathbf{Y}_1^{\mathbf{3D}}, \mathbf{Z}_1^{\mathbf{3D}}$).

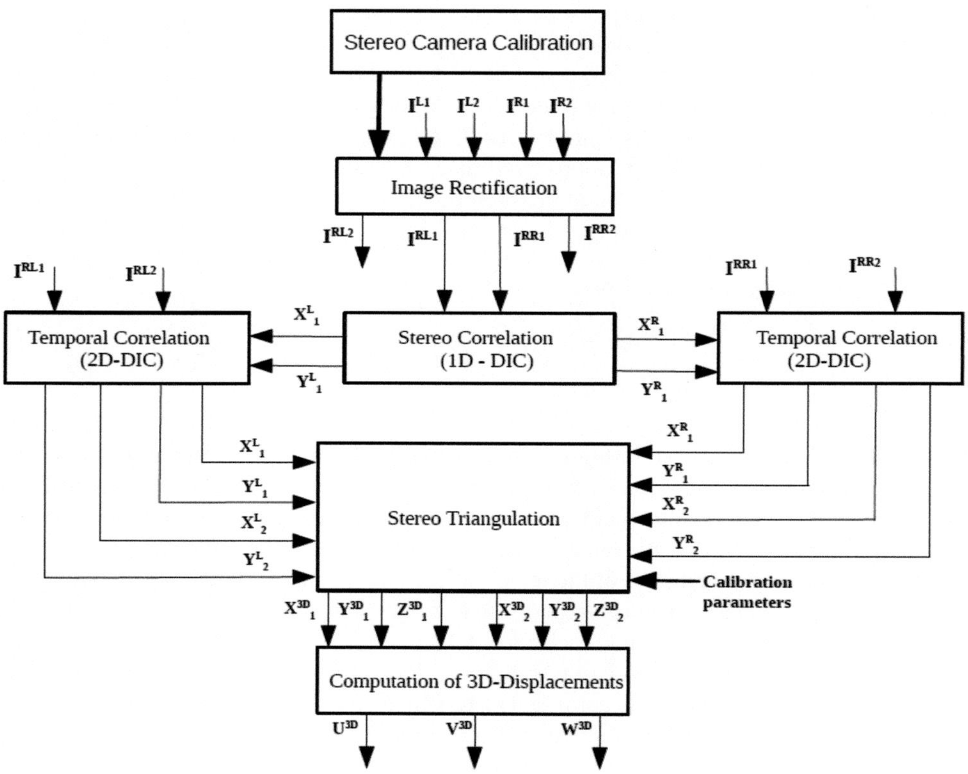

Fig. 1 Computation flow of image processing using Stereo-DIC technique with two stereo image pairs.

Nomenclature:

- $\mathbf{I}^{\mathbf{RL}_1}, \mathbf{I}^{\mathbf{RR}_1}$: Rectified image pairs of reference stereo image pair ($\mathbf{I}^{\mathbf{L1}}, \mathbf{I}^{\mathbf{R1}}$)
- $\mathbf{I}^{\mathbf{RL}_2}, \mathbf{I}^{\mathbf{RR}_2}$: Rectified image pairs of deformed stereo image pair ($\mathbf{I}^{\mathbf{L2}}, \mathbf{I}^{\mathbf{R2}}$)

[1] terminology used in CUDA programming model, https://developer.nvidia.com/cuda-toolkit

- $\mathbf{X_1^L, Y_1^L, X_1^R, Y_1^R}$: Correspondence points after stereo correlation step in spatial domain
- $\mathbf{X_2^L, Y_2^L}$: Correspondence points after left temporal correlation step in spatial domain
- $\mathbf{X_2^R, Y_2^R}$: Correspondence points after right temporal correlation step in spatial domain
- $\mathbf{X_1^{3D}, Y_1^{3D}, Z_1^{3D}}$: Reference surface re-projected after stereo triangulation step of $(\mathbf{X_1^L, Y_1^L, X_1^R, Y_1^R})$
- $\mathbf{X_2^{3D}, Y_2^{3D}, Z_2^{3D}}$: Deformed surface re-projected after stereo triangulation step of $(\mathbf{X_2^L, Y_2^L, X_2^R, Y_2^R})$
- $\mathbf{U^{3D}, V^{3D}, W^{3D}}$: Full-field displacement vectors in 3D

The matrix representation to compute the 3D position of any point, $\tilde{\mathbf{X}} = (\mathbf{X}, \mathbf{Y}, \mathbf{Z})$ in the left camera is written as below. This typically involves solving a system of linear equations.

$$[\mathbf{V}]_{\mathbf{4\times3}}\{\tilde{\mathbf{X}}\}_{3\times1} = \{\mathbf{r}\}_{4\times1} \tag{1}$$

where,

$$[\mathbf{V}]_{\mathbf{4\times3}} = \begin{bmatrix} f_x^L & 0 & (x^L - c_x^L) \\ 0 & f_y^L & (y^L - c_y^L) \\ -f_x^R & 0 & (x^R - c_x^R) \\ 0 & f_y^R & (y^R - c_y^R) \end{bmatrix} \tag{2}$$

$$\{\mathbf{r}\}_{\mathbf{4\times1}} = \begin{bmatrix} 0 \\ 0 \\ -f_x^R T \\ 0 \end{bmatrix} \tag{3}$$

The elements of the matrix $\mathbf{V}$ represent intrinsics parameters that are derived from the camera calibration process. In this context, f_x^L and f_y^L represent the focal lengths of the left camera along the $\mathbf{x}$ and $\mathbf{y}$ axes, respectively. Similarly, c_x^L and c_y^L denote the principal point of the left camera along the $\mathbf{x}$ and $\mathbf{y}$ axes. For the right camera, f_x^R and f_y^R represent the focal lengths along the $\mathbf{x}$ and $\mathbf{y}$ axes, respectively, while c_x^R and c_y^R represent the principal point of the right camera along the $\mathbf{x}$ and $\mathbf{y}$ axes. Next, the vector $\{\mathbf{r}\}$ is a 4×1 column vector, which is related to the translation between the stereo camera pair. The solution of the above system of equations is obtained by the linear least square method represented in Equation 4 below:

$$\{\tilde{\mathbf{X}}_1^{\mathbf{L}}\} = [\mathbf{V^T V}]^{-1}[\mathbf{V}]^{\mathbf{T}}\mathbf{r} \tag{4}$$

Next, equation 5 is used to transform a point $\{\tilde{\mathbf{X}}_1^{\mathbf{L}}\}$ in the left camera coordinate system to the right camera coordinate system.

$$\{\tilde{\mathbf{X}}_2^{\mathbf{R}}\} = \mathbf{R}\{\tilde{\mathbf{X}}_1^{\mathbf{L}}\} + \mathrm{T} \tag{5}$$

Here, the rotation ($\mathbf{R}$) matrix and translation ($\mathbf{T}$) vector describes the rotation as well as translation of the left camera coordinate system relative to the right camera coordinate system. These are the extrinsic parameters calculated during the camera calibration process. By repeating the above process for multiple points in the stereo correlated images, 3D surface(s) of the object in its undeformed and deformed states is reconstructed. It is well known that the stereo rectification process simplifies the number of intrinsic parameters by removing distortion. Thus, the orientation of right camera with respect to left camera is represented by an identity matrix as in Equation 6. In a similar way, the translation between the cameras in the rectified stereo rig is represented by a vector $\mathbf{T}$ as given in equation 7.

$$[\mathbf{R}] = \begin{bmatrix} 1 & 0 & 0 \\ 0 & 1 & 0 \\ 0 & 0 & 1 \end{bmatrix} \tag{6}$$

$$[\mathbf{T}] = \begin{bmatrix} \mathbf{T_x} \\ \mathbf{T_y} \\ \mathbf{T_z} \end{bmatrix} = \begin{bmatrix} \mathbf{T}[1,1] \\ \mathbf{T}[2,1] \\ \mathbf{T}[3,1] \end{bmatrix} \tag{7}$$

Typically, the stereo triangulation process can be viewed as a structure/shape reconstruction problem. Here, the point correspondences estimated by using stereo correlation step is projected to determine the point(s) of intersection (i.e., 3D points). It can be understood that the number of times the stereo triangulation process is repeated is same as the number of stereo rectified image pairs available during post processing. If there are $\mathtt{t}$ corresponding points between rectified stereo images $\mathbf{I^{RL_1}}$ and $\mathbf{I^{RL_2}}$, re-projection of the 3D points is given by the Equation 8.

Input: $\mathbf{X_1^L}, \mathbf{Y_1^L}, \mathbf{X_1^R}, \mathbf{Y_1^R}, \mathbf{c_x^L}, \mathbf{c_y^L}, \mathbf{c_x^R}, \mathbf{c_y^R}, \mathbf{f_x^L}, \mathbf{f_y^L}, \mathbf{f_x^R}, \mathbf{f_y^R}, \mathbf{R}, \mathbf{T}$

Output: $\mathbf{X_1^{3D}}, \mathbf{Y_1^{3D}}, \mathbf{Z_1^{3D}}$

for $i \leftarrow 1$ **to** t **do**

$\quad \mathrm{x_t[1,i]} = \frac{\mathrm{X_1^L[1,i]} - c_x^L}{f_x^L}$ ▷ Left camera - homogeneous coordinates

$\quad \mathrm{x_t[2,i]} = \frac{\mathrm{Y_1^L[1,i]} - c_y^L}{f_y^L}$

$\quad \mathrm{x_t[3,i]} = 1.0$

$\quad \mathrm{x_{tt}[1,i]} = \frac{\mathrm{X_1^R[1,i]} - c_x^R}{f_x^R}$ ▷ Right camera - homogeneous coordinates

$\quad \mathrm{x_{tt}[2,i]} = \frac{\mathrm{Y_1^R[1,i]} - c_y^R}{f_y^R}$

$\quad \mathrm{x_{tt}[3,i]} = 1.0$

$\quad \mathrm{u[1:3,i]} = \sum_{\mathrm{m}=1}^{3} (\mathrm{R[1:3,m]} * \mathrm{x_t[m,i]})$

$\quad \mathrm{nx_{t2}[1,i]} = \sum_{\mathrm{m}=1}^{3} (\mathrm{x_t[m,i]})^2$

$\quad \mathrm{nx_{tt2}[1,i]} = \sum_{\mathrm{m}=1}^{3} (\mathrm{x_{tt}[m,i]})^2 + \mathrm{u[3,i]} * \mathrm{x_{tt}[3,i]}$

$\quad \mathrm{DD[1,i]} = (\mathrm{nx_{t2}[1,i]} * \mathrm{nx_{tt2}[1,i]}) - \{\sum_{\mathrm{m}=1}^{3} (\mathrm{u[m,i]} * \mathrm{x_{tt}[m,i]})\}$

$\quad \mathrm{u_T[1,i]} = \sum_{\mathrm{m}=1}^{3} (\mathrm{u[m,i]} * \mathrm{T[m,1]})$

$\quad \mathrm{x_{ttT}[1,i]} = \sum_{\mathrm{m}=1}^{3} (\mathrm{x_{tt}[m,i]} * \mathrm{T[m,1]})$

$\quad \mathrm{x_{ttu}[1,i]} = \sum_{\mathrm{m}=1}^{3} (\mathrm{u[m,i]} * \mathrm{x_{tt}[m,1]})$

$\quad \mathrm{NN_1[1,i]} = (\mathrm{x_{ttu}[1,i]} * \mathrm{x_{ttT}[1,i]}) - (\mathrm{nx_{tt2}[1,i]} * \mathrm{u_T[1,i]})$

$\quad \mathrm{NN_2[1,i]} = (\mathrm{nx_{t2}[1,i]} * \mathrm{x_{ttT}[1,i]}) - (\mathrm{u_T[1,i]} * \mathrm{x_{ttu}[1,i]})$

$\quad \mathrm{Z_t[1,i]} = \frac{\mathrm{NN1[1,i]}}{\mathrm{DD[1,i]}}$

$\quad \mathrm{Z_{tt2}[1,i]} = \frac{\mathrm{NN2[1,i]}}{\mathrm{DD[1,i]}}$

$\quad \mathrm{X_1[1:3,i]} = \mathrm{x_t[1:3,i]} * \mathrm{Z_t[1:3,i]}$

$\quad \mathrm{X_2[1:3,i]} = \sum_{\mathrm{j}=1}^{3} \mathrm{R[j,i]} * \mathrm{X_1[j,1:3]} + \mathrm{T[j,1]}$

$\quad \mathrm{X_L[1:3,i]} = \frac{\mathrm{X_1[1:3,i]} + \mathrm{X_2[1:3,i]}}{2}$

$\quad \mathbf{X_1^{3D}[1,i]} = \mathrm{X_L[1,i]}$

$\quad \mathbf{Y_1^{3D}[1,i]} = \mathrm{X_L[2,i]}$

$\quad \mathbf{Z_1^{3D}[1,i]} = \mathrm{X_L[3,i]}$

end

Algorithm 1: Pseudo-code for stereo triangulation between $\mathbf{I^{RL_1}}$ and $\mathbf{I^{RR_1}}$ using `Sequential version`

$$\{\mathbf{X^L}\} = \begin{bmatrix} \mathbf{X_1^{3D}} \\ \mathbf{Y_1^{3D}} \\ \mathbf{Z_1^{3D}} \end{bmatrix} \tag{8}$$

The pseudo-code for stereo triangulation between $\mathbf{I^{RL_1}}$ and $\mathbf{I^{RR_1}}$ is presented as Algorithm 1. This open source implementation is based on the camera calibration toolbox for Matlab by Jean-Yves Bouguet.[2] The inputs to this module are

[2]http://robots.stanford.edu/cs223b04/JeanYvesCalib/.

spatial point correspondences, focal length, principal points, rotation matrix and translation vector values. A for loop is initialized at line 4 for `t` subsets between images $\mathbf{I}^{\mathbf{RL_1}}$ and $\mathbf{I}^{\mathbf{RR_1}}$ to compute triangulated points corresponding to the reference surface as the output. At the end of the first iteration, this results in a 3D point for the first subset ($\mathbf{X}_1^{\mathbf{3D}}[1,1]$, $\mathbf{Y}_1^{\mathbf{3D}}[\mathbf{1},\mathbf{1}]$, $\mathbf{Z}_1^{\mathbf{3D}}[\mathbf{1},\mathbf{1}]$). Line 5 to line 25 represent the sequence of calculations during an iteration cycle. After initialization of `for` loop, the first step is to normalize the image projections in homogeneous coordinates as represented by line 5 upto line 10. Next, equations 4 and 5 are implemented by line 10 upto line 23. Finally, this process is repeated for `t` iterations.

Analysis

The pseudo-code to reconstruct a 3D surface (single reference and multiple deformed surface(s)) using a GPU is presented as Algorithm 2. In this pseudo-code, three kernels are launched to transform the calculations run using CPU onto a GPU. The first kernel is responsible to normalize the spatial coordinates of left camera ranging from line 4 to line 9. Likewise, code from line 10 to line 14 is used to normalize the coordinates of the right camera. Here, the focus of the third kernel is to calculate the 3D object point corresponding to each subset in a given stereo image pair. It is observed that this step has massive scope for data parallelism (i.e. `intra-parallelism`, `inter-parallelism` and `inter-image parallelism`). It is made feasible by storing the spatial coordinates of the point correspondences between $\mathbf{I}^{\mathbf{RL_1}}$ and $\mathbf{I}^{\mathbf{RL_2}}$ together with point correspondences between $\mathbf{I}^{\mathbf{RR_1}}$ and $\mathbf{I}^{\mathbf{RR_2}}$ in the global memory of the GPU thereby enabling simultaneous data access by individual processor cores. As mentioned earlier, a stereo triangulation step is executed two times during processing of two stereo image pairs as per the stereo-DIC algorithm. The first stereo triangulation step is useful to re-project a reference surface of the specimen. The second invocation of triangulation step is responsible to reconstruct the deformed surface of the specimen. Because of the data independent nature of calculations within the stereo triangulation module, it is evident that its computation speed shall improve by mapping the steps to hardware resources of the GPU.

Before presenting the results for stereo-DIC computation, we present the configuration details of the framework used to test the stereo image pairs. In this study, the heterogeneous framework comprises of Intel Xeon octa-core CPU and NVIDIA Tesla K20C GPU. The software package utilized to read digital images and implement `sequential version` of the stereo-DIC algorithm is developed using MATLAB R2017a.

To study the performance of the stereo-triangulation algorithm, `Stereo Sample 1 (35mm - Experimental images)` dataset from Stereo DIC challenge repository [3] is considered. This dataset consists of experimental images with resolution of 2048×2448 pixels. In this research work, the stereo images are used after rectification of stereo pairs. For the purpose of this experiment, a ROI in both $\mathbf{I}^{\mathbf{RL_1}}$ and $\mathbf{I}^{\mathbf{RR_1}}$ is selected as shown in Figure 2. Firstly, stereo correlation module is executed between reference stereo image pairs ($\mathrm{I}^{\mathrm{RL_1}}$ and $\mathbf{I}^{\mathbf{RR_1}}$).

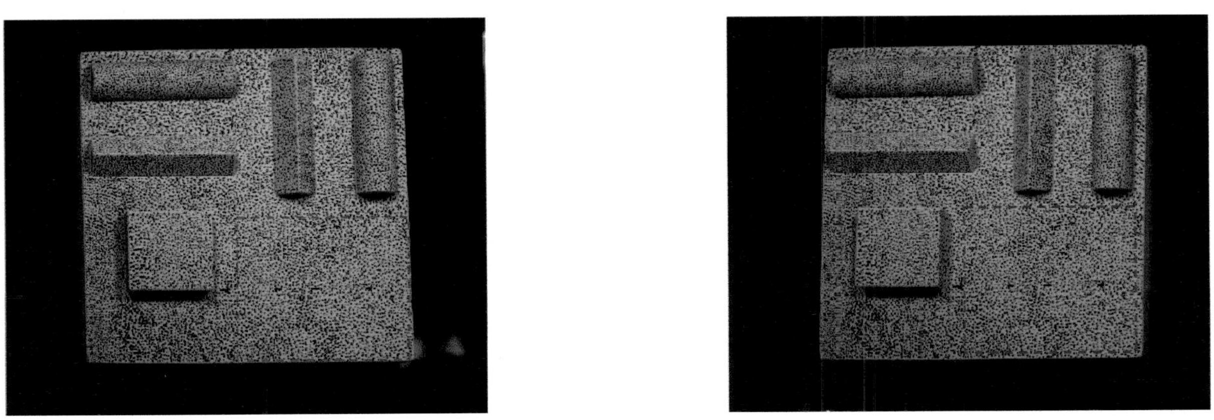

Fig. 2 Stereo Sample 1 dataset from DIC Challenge Repository: (a) Rectified left reference image ($\mathrm{I}^{\mathrm{RL_1}}$) with a chosen region-of-interest, (b) Rectified right reference image ($\mathrm{I}^{\mathrm{RR_1}}$) of undeformed specimen.

[3] https://idics.org/challenge/

The average timing results for stereo triangulation of reference surface with 437 subsets using `heterogeneous version` is 17.43 milliseconds (inclusive of data transfer overhead) and 0.30 milliseconds (exclusive of data transfer overhead). This implies that the speedup factor shall improve with increase in the number of subsets.

Input: $\mathbf{X_1^L}$, $\mathbf{Y_1^L}$, $\mathbf{X_1^R}$, $\mathbf{Y_1^R}$, $\mathbf{c_x^L}$, $\mathbf{c_y^L}$, $\mathbf{c_x^R}$, $\mathbf{c_y^R}$, $\mathbf{f_x^L}$, $\mathbf{f_y^L}$, $\mathbf{f_x^R}$, $\mathbf{f_y^R}$, **R**, **T**

Output: $\mathbf{X_1^{3D}}$, $\mathbf{Y_1^{3D}}$, $\mathbf{Z_1^{3D}}$

for *$(t \times N)$ parallel threads* **do**

tid = getThreadId() ▷ `Intra-parallelism and Inter-parallelism`

$\mathrm{x_t[2*tid] = (X_1^L[2*tid] - c_x^L[0])/f_x^L[0]}$

$\mathrm{x_t[(2*tid)+1] = (Y_1^L[(2*tid)+1] - c_y^L[0])/f_y^L[0]}$

$\mathrm{xt[0] = x_t[2*tid]}$

$\mathrm{xt[1] = x_t[(2*tid)+1]}$

$\mathrm{xt[2] = 1.0f}$

$\mathrm{x_{tt}[2*tid] = (X_1^R[2*tid] - c_x^R[0])/f_x^R[0]}$

$\mathrm{x_{tt}[(2*tid)+1] = (Y_1^R[(2*tid)+1] - c_y^R[0])/f_y^R[0]}$

$\mathrm{xtt[0] = x_{tt}[2*tid]}$

$\mathrm{xtt[1] = x_{tt}[(2*tid)+1]}$

$\mathrm{xtt[2] = 1.0f}$

$\mathrm{u[0] = (R[0]*xt[0]) + (R[3]*xt[1]) + (R[6]*xt[2])}$

$\mathrm{u[1] = (R[1]*xt[0]) + (R[4]*xt[1]) + (R[7]*xt[2])}$

$\mathrm{u[2] = (R[2]*xt[0]) + (R[5]*xt[1]) + (R[8]*xt[2])}$

$\mathrm{nx_{t2} = (xt[0])^2 + (xt[1])^2 + (xt[2])^2}$

$\mathrm{nx_{tt2} = (xtt[0])^2 + (xtt[1])^2 + (xtt[2])^2}$

$\mathrm{DD = (nx_{t2}*nx_{tt2}) - \{(u[0]*xtt[0]) + (u[1]*xtt[1]) + (u[2]*xtt[2])\}^2}$

$\mathrm{u_T = \sum_{m=0}^{2} (u[m]*T[m])}$

$\mathrm{x_{ttT} = \sum_{m=0}^{2} (xtt[m]*T[m])}$

$\mathrm{x_{ttu} = \sum_{m=0}^{2} (u[m]*xtt[m])}$

$\mathrm{NN1 = (xttu*xttT) - (nx_{tt2}*u_T)}$

$\mathrm{NN2 = (nx_{t2}*x_{ttT}) - (nx_{tt2}*u_T)}$

Algorithm 2: Pseudo-code for stereo triangulation between $\mathbf{I^{RL_1}}$ and $\mathbf{I^{RR_1}}$ in stereoDIC computation realized using GPU (`Heterogeneous version`)

continued ...

for *$(t \times N)$ parallel threads* **do**

$Z_t = \frac{NN1}{DD}$

$Z_{tt} = \frac{NN2}{DD}$

$X_1[0] = xt[0] * Z_t$

$X_1[1] = xt[1] * Z_t$

$X_1[2] = xt[2] * Z_t$

$diff_{new}[0] = (xtt[0] * Z_{tt}) - T[0]$

$diff_{new}[1] = (xtt[1] * Z_{tt}) - T[1]$

$diff_{new}[2] = (xtt[2] * Z_{tt}) - T[2]$

$R^{'} = transpose(R)$

$X_2[0] = (R^{'}[0] * diff_{new}[0]) + (R^{'}[3] * diff_{new}[1]) + (R^{'}[6] * diff_{new}[2])$

$X_2[1] = (R^{'}[1] * diff_{new}[0]) + (R^{'}[4] * diff_{new}[1]) + (R^{'}[7] * diff_{new}[2])$

$X_2[2] = (R^{'}[2] * diff_{new}[0]) + (R^{'}[5] * diff_{new}[1]) + (R^{'}[8] * diff_{new}[2])$

$X_L[0] = (X_1[0] + X_2[0])/2$

$X_L[1] = (X_1[1] + X_2[1])/2$

$X_L[2] = (X_1[2] + X_2[2])/2$

$\mathbf{X_1^{3D}}[\mathbf{tid}] = X_L[0]$

$\mathbf{Y_1^{3D}}[\mathbf{tid}] = X_L[1]$

$\mathbf{Z_1^{3D}}[\mathbf{tid}] = X_L[2]$

Algorithm 2: Pseudo-code for stereo triangulation between $\mathbf{I}^{\mathbf{RL_1}}$ and $\mathbf{I}^{\mathbf{RR_1}}$ in stereoDIC computation realized using GPU (in `Heterogeneous version`)

- `reference surface` 36.82 milli seconds
- `deformed surface` 11.94 milli seconds

The proposed heterogeneous framework also implements the pseudo-code presented in Algorithm 2. As discussed earlier, the stereo triangulation is implemented to explore both `intra-parallelism` and `inter-parallelism`. Table 1 presents average computation times in milliseconds for different pixel counts (from 1 to 10,000,000) are compared across CPU, GPU_1, and GPU_2 implementations. As pixel count increases, the computation time on the CPU remains signifi-

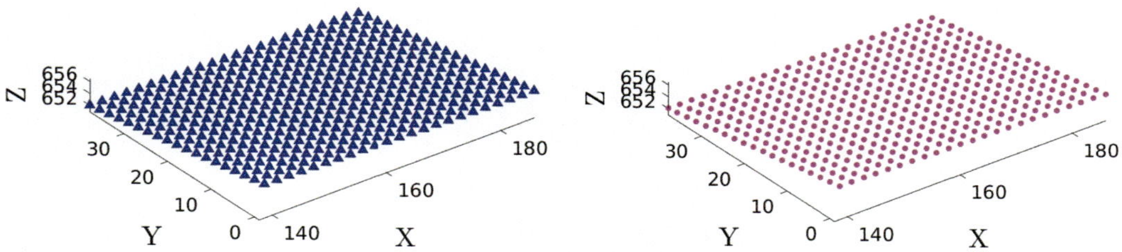

Fig. 3 Stereo triangulation of reference surface computed using (a) `Sequential` and (b) `Heterogeneous version`.

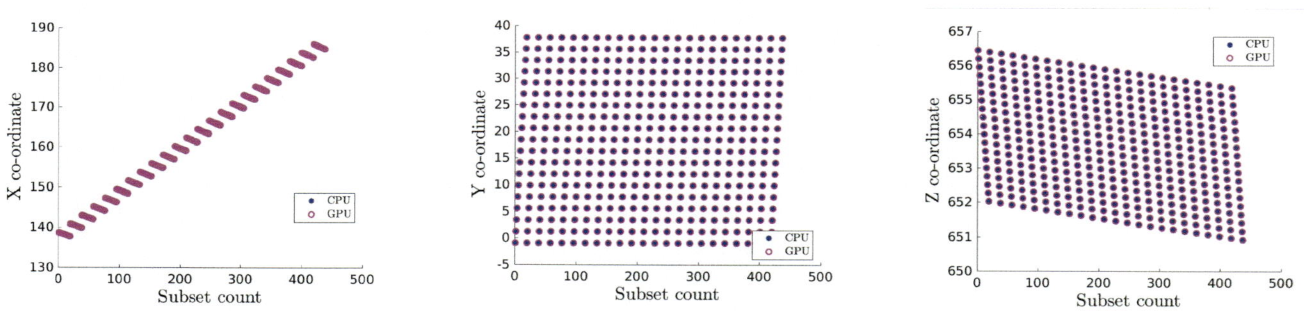

Fig. 4 Stereo triangulation : Compare 3-D co-ordinates of reference surface along (a) X-direction, (b) Y-direction , (c) Z-direction computed using `Sequential version` and `Heterogeneous version`

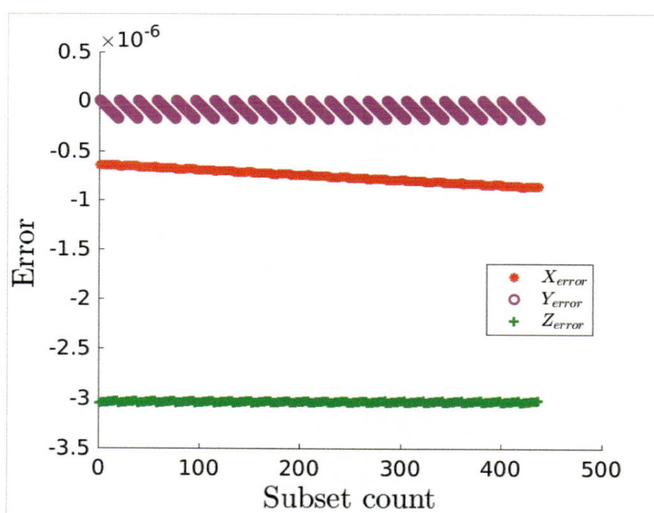

Fig. 5 Stereo triangulation of reference surface : Error between `Sequential` and `Heterogeneous version`

cantly higher than that on the GPUs. The speedup factors illustrate substantial performance improvements, particularly with GPU_{25}, where speedup factor reaches up to $758.4\times$ for smaller pixel counts. However, as the pixel count increases to $10,000,000$, the speedup factors drop to approximately $1.8\times$, indicating diminishing returns due to data transfer overhead. Overall, the results underscore the efficiency of heterogeneous processing, particularly for smaller pixel counts, while also highlighting the impact of data transfer overhead on performance.

Table 1 Stereo triangulation - Impact of data transfer overhead : Pixel count versus computation time and speedup factor (inclusive and exclusive of data transfer overhead) specifically realized using `sequential` and `heterogeneous` version.

Number of pixels	Average computation time (in milli seconds)			Speedup factor	
	CPU	GPU_1[4]	GPU_2[5]	S_1[6]	S_2[7]
1	221.7	16.7	0.3	13.3×	749.3×
50	225.3	16.8	0.3	13.4×	758.4×
100	228.5	16.8	0.3	13.6×	720.5×
500	227.3	16.4	0.3	13.9×	730.2×
1000	237.5	16.7	0.3	14.2×	729.9×
5000	234.8	19.4	0.3	12.1×	724.3×
10000	223.7	20.1	0.3	11.1×	732.9×
50000	224.6	23.6	0.4	9.5×	548.5×
100000	224.0	28.8	1.0	7.8×	232.9×
5000000	995.9	511.4	8.1	1.9×	123.4×
10000000	1757.7	991.7	15.1	1.8×	116.5×

[GPU_{14}, S_{16}] Including data transfer overhead
[GPU_{25}, S_{27}] Excluding data transfer overhead

Conclusion

To summarize, this paper addresses the parallelization approach followed to improve the computation speed of a stereo triangulation algorithm. By increasing the total number of spatial co-ordinates to be triangulated from 50 to 10,000, it is observed that by using `heterogeneous` framework, the overall speedup factor of the stereo triangulation step improves by $\approx 758\times$ to $\approx 232\times$. It also highlights the impact of data transfer overhead on the overall gain in speedup factor. Another advantage of the proposed framework is that it is modular, scalable, and can be easily ported on to other NVIDIA-based GPU cards.

Acknowledgments Indian Institute of Technology Madras and Krea University, India.

References

1. R. I. Hartley and P. Sturm. Triangulation. *In International Conference on Computer Analysis of Images and Patterns, Springer, Berlin, Heidelberg*, pages 190–197, 1995.
2. M. A. Sutton, J. J. Orteu, and H. Schreier. Image correlation for shape, motion and deformation measurements: basic concepts, theory and applications. 2009.
3. M.A. Sutton and F. Hild. Recent advances and perspectives in digital image correlation. *Experimental Mechanics*, 55:1–8, 2015.
4. Mullai Thiagu, Sankara J Subramanian, and Rupesh Nasre. Fast, sub-pixel accurate digital image correlation algorithm powered by heterogeneous (cpu-gpu) framework. In *Advancement of Optical Methods & Digital Image Correlation in Experimental Mechanics, Volume 3: Proceedings of the 2018 Annual Conference on Experimental and Applied Mechanics*, pages 95–102. Springer, 2019.
5. Mullai Thiagu, Sankara J Subramanian, and Rupesh Nasre. High-speed, two-dimensional digital image correlation algorithm using heterogeneous (CPU-GPU) framework. *Strain*, 56(3):e12342, 2020.

Chapter 5
A Sublimation-based Pattern Generation Technique for Deformation Analysis of Additively Manufactured Specimens

Nicolas A. Yusim, Angel Matos-De Los Santos, Austin M. Giordano, and Fu-Pen Chiang

Abstract A deformation analysis method is proposed for additively manufactured (AM) specimens, utilizing sublimated speckles for analysis Computer-Aided Speckle Interferometry (CASI). This approach allows precise control over the size and density of the sublimated patterns, which are integrated into the surface of the AM specimen through the heat and pressure applied during the fused deposition modeling (FDM) 3D printing process. This technique creates the speckle pattern without altering the specimen's integrity. The sublimation-deposited speckle patterns facilitate the exploration of various pattern-generation methods (e.g., pseudo-random, Goodman) to identify the optimal speckle pattern. The material behaviors of the speckled and un-speckled specimens are characterized and compared to determine the impact of the speckle pattern on the specimen's material properties.

Keywords Speckle · Additive manufacturing · Sublimation · DIC (Digital Images Correlation)

Introduction

Additive manufacturing (AM) is an extremely lucrative industry valued at 20.37 billion USD in 2023 and expected to grow to a 88.28 billion-dollar industry by 2030 [1]. This rapid industry growth is due in part to AM's continuously improving ability to manufacture consumer grade, end use products [2]. These improvements come in many forms such as new materials, modifications to the current manufacturing method, and modifications to tool path generation algorithms [3]. With the swift inclusion of AM parts into many consumer products comes an inherent need to validate their structural performance to ensure safe and effective use by the consumer.

In this paper, an alternative method of applying a fully customizable deformation pattern of choice onto a specimen manufacturing with Fused Deposition Modeling (FDM) is presented. This method uses sublimation paper which is able to transfer ink onto a surface through use of heat and pressure [4]. By applying the sublimation paper onto the heated surface where the specimen is manufactured, the pattern is transferred without altering any material properties on the surface while maintaining the resolution of the pattern. The deformation analysis method technique chosen to evaluate this method is Computer Aided Speckle Interferometry (CASI) [5] due to its ubiquity within the experimental mechanics field. This was combined with FDM printing since the heated manufacturing surface provides substantial heat to successfully sublimate the pattern into the specimen.

Speckle theory

Speckles are generated when an opaque surface is illuminated by a coherent light source, such as a laser. Wavelets from the laser are reflected off of the surface and interfere with each other at a chosen plane of focus to create a speckle pattern as shown in Fig. 1 a [5, 6, 7]. This interference results in a laser speckle pattern similar to the one shown in Fig. 1 b.

Nicolas A. Yusim · Angel Matos-De Los Santos · Austin M. Giordano · Fu-Pen Chiang
Laboratory for Experimental Mechanics Research, Department of Mechanical Engineering at Stony Brook University, Stony Brook, NY 11794-2300, USA.
e-mail: nicolas.yusim@stonybrook.edu; angel.matos-delossantos@stonybrook.edu; austin.giordano@stonybrook.edu; fu-pen.chiang@stonybrook.edu

Chi-Hung Hwang et al. (eds.), *Advancement of Optical Methods & Digital Image Correlation in Experimental Mechanics, Vol. 2*, Conference Proceedings
of the Society for Experimental Mechanics Series, https://doi.org/10.13052/9788743808282-5

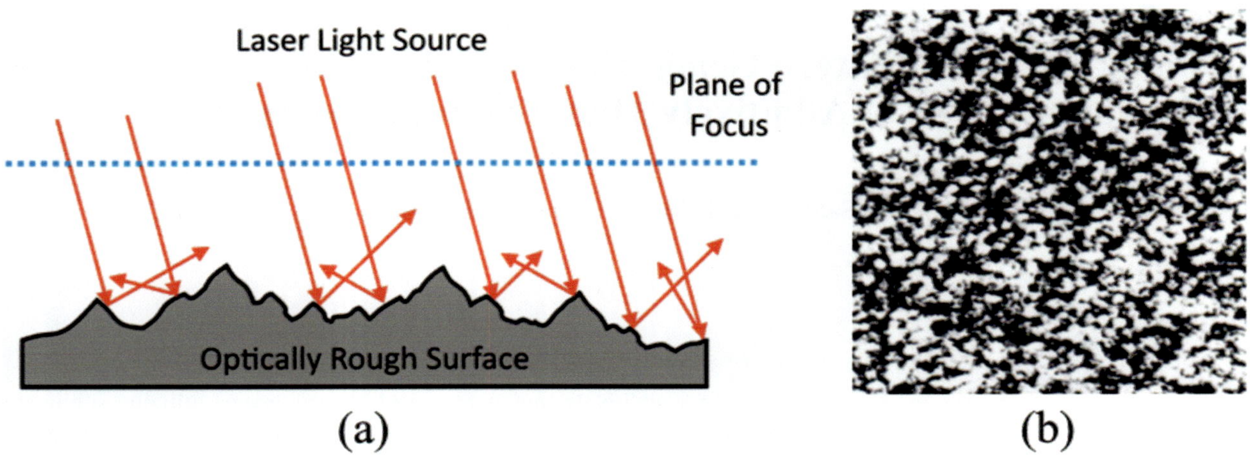

Fig. 1 (a) Graphical representation of laser wavelet interference next to (b) enlarged view of laser speckles

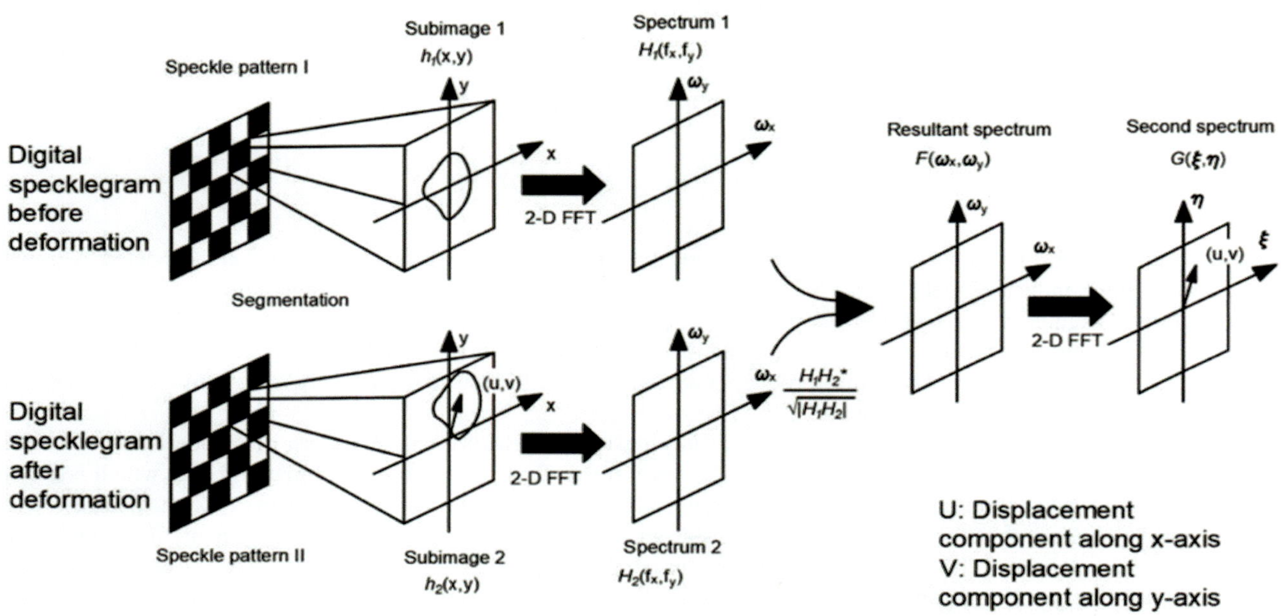

Fig. 2 Computer Aided Speckle Interferometry Algorithm

Speckle interferometry was simultaneously developed into two digital methods, Digital Image Correlation (DIC) and CASI; The fundamental difference between the two being that DIC matches a kernel of speckles to its deformed location to get displacements while CASI uses optical processing techniques to obtain displacements [6, 7]. The CASI Algorithm is shown below in Fig. 2.

The digitization of speckle interferometry has led to the development of multiple pattern generation techniques to simulate the naturally occurring laser speckle pattern. Some examples of these pattern generations techniques include the Pseudo-Random pattern and the Goodman pattern among others. Examples of the Pseudo-Random pattern, the Goodman pattern, and laser generated speckles are shown below in Fig. 3.

The Pseudo-Random pattern generates a grid of random black and white pixels using a built-in MATLAB function [8], while the Goodman pattern is a mathematical representation of laser speckle interference made by generating random phasors in a table in accordance with the equation below [9]:

$$e^{(2i\pi \cdot rand)} \tag{1}$$

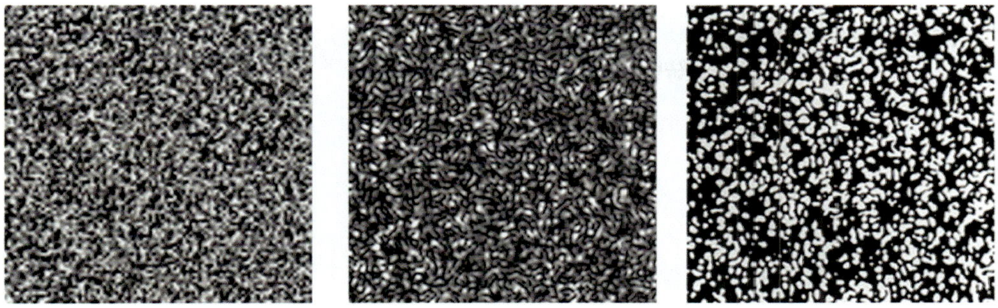

(a) (b) (c)

Fig. 3 (a) Pseudo-Randomly generated speckle pattern, (b) Goodman generated speckle pattern, (c) laser generated speckle pattern

Sample Preparation

Specimens presented in this paper were manufactured in accordance with ASTM D638-14 standard for tensile properties of plastics using white poly lactic acid (PLA). A MATLAB program was developed to produce a Goodman pattern with a speckle size of 8 pixels for the maximum capacity of the inkjet printer used. In this paper the print resolution of the inkjet printer is limited by its minimum axis resolution of 1440 dpi. An initial Goodman pattern was generated with 16384 × 16384 pixels, which is then cropped to 16200 × 11880 pixels. This pattern was printed onto sublimation paper as shown in Fig. 4 below.

Fig. 4 Specimen with Goodman generated speckle pattern sublimated onto its surface

The sublimation paper is then adhered to the heated build plate of a Prusa Mk4S so that the specimen can be printed on top of the sublimation paper. A Prusa Mk4S was used due to its adaptive bed leveling procedure, which is capable of adjusting to any existing surface on the build plate to manufacture the specimen. As the printer deposits the heated PLA onto the paper, the ink is sublimated onto the surface of the first layer. A microscope image of the Goodman pattern on the specimen is shown in Fig. 5 a, with the sublimation paper shown after use in Fig. 5 b.

(a)

Fig. 5 *Continued.*

(b)

Fig. 5 (a) Microscope image of speckle pattern on printed specimen (b) Sublimation paper on printer after specimens were removed

Experimental Procedure and Analysis

Each specimen was affixed into a universal testing machine, and loaded in tension with a displacement control of 0.5 mm/min. Each specimen was imaged with a Canon EOS 5DSR to be analyzed. The CASI results are presented in Fig. 6 and the resulting force-displacement plots of blank, and sublimated speckled specimens are shown in Fig. 7 below.

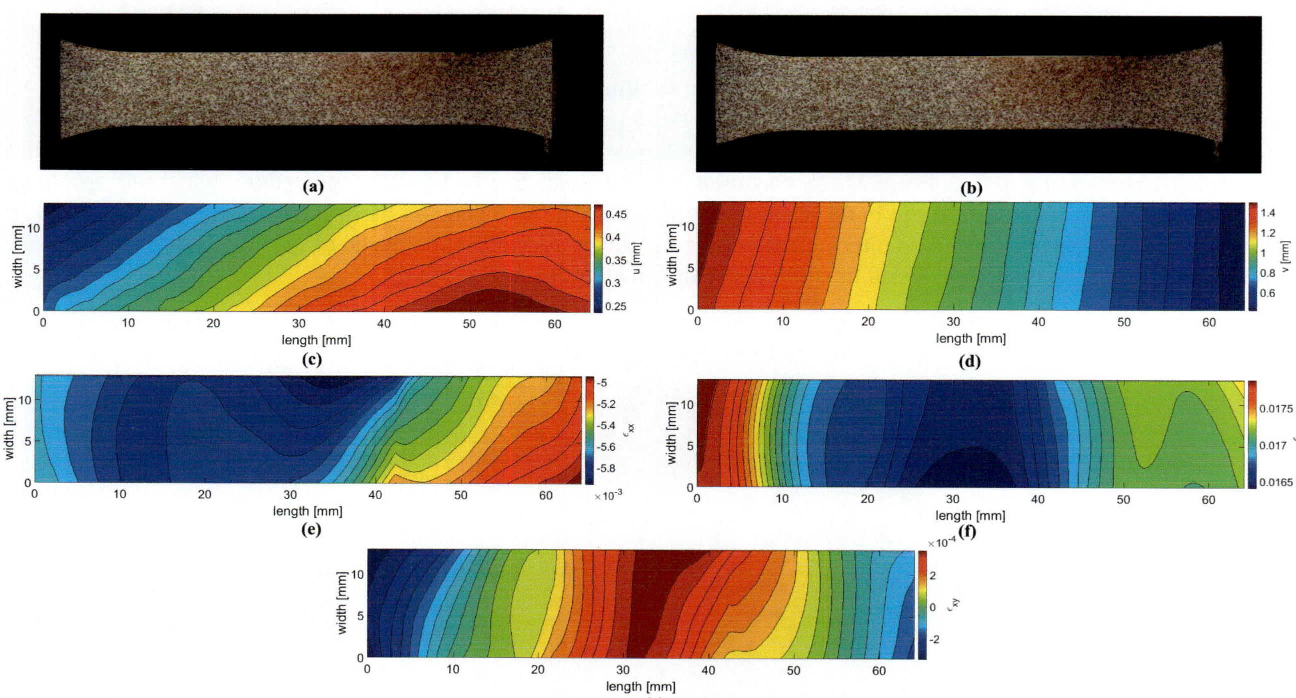

Fig. 6 (a) Undeformed specimen, (b) deformed specimen, (c) u-displacement field, (d) v-displacement field, (e) ϵ_{xx} field, (f)) ϵ_{yy} field, (g)) ϵ_{xy} field.

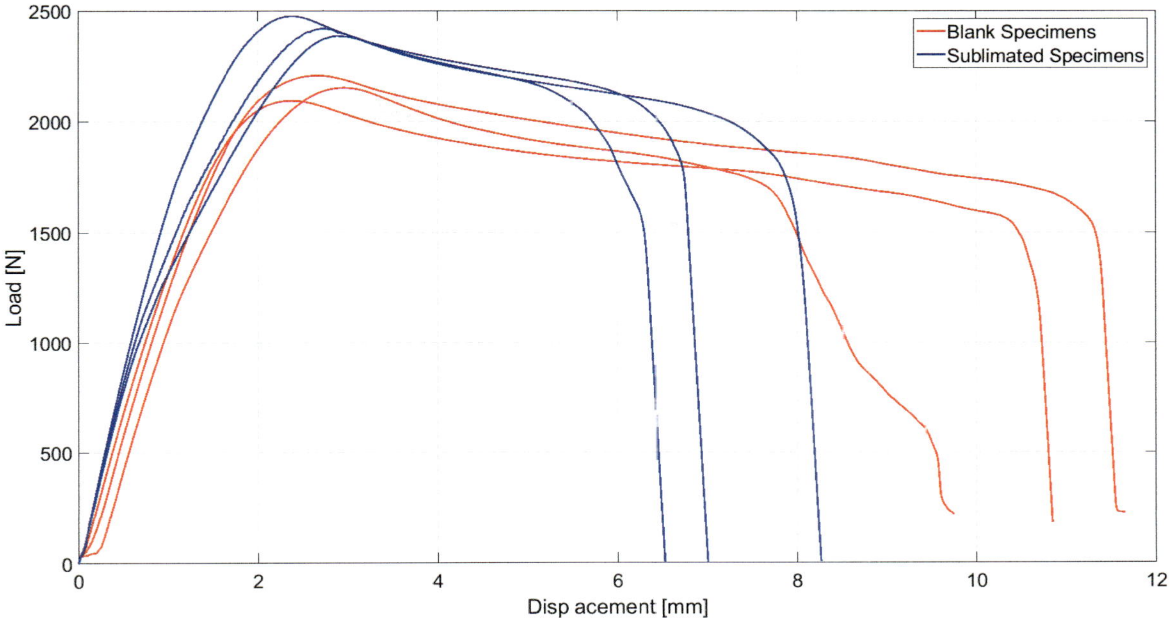

Fig. 7 Force-displacement graph of specimens with sublimated speckles compared to blank specimens

Conclusion

We have produced accurate displacement fields from CASI analysis of additively manufactured specimens with sublimated speckles. We find that speckled specimens produce similar results in the force-displacement when compared to blank specimens. In previous work [10], it was seen that printing a speckle pattern using a multi-material printing technique lead to limit plasticity of the specimen, the technique present in this work does not have that drawback. This work can be extended by utilizing the technique shown to produce a moiré pattern which will enable analyze via the sampling moiré method [11]. Further work needs to be done to determine the viability of the experimental technique shown, but from these initial results, producing specimens with sublimated patterns for deformation analysis appears to be promising.

References

1. Grand View Research, "Additive Manufacturing Market Size & Trends," 2024. [Online]. Available: https://www.grandviewresearch.com/industry-analysis/additive-manufacturing-market
2. Z. Zhu, P. Pradel, R. Bibb, and J. Moultrie, "A Framework for Designing End Use Products for Direct Manufacturing Using Additive Manufacturing Technologies," Aug. 2017.
3. D. Syrlybayev, B. Zharylkassyn, A. Seisekulova, M. Akhmetov, A. Perveen, and D. Talamona, "Optimisation of strength properties of FDM printed parts—A critical review," May 01, 2021, *MDPI AG*. doi: 10.3390/polym13101587.
4. E. Toshikj and B. Prangoski, "Textile Sublimation Printing: Impact of Total Ink Limiting Level and Sublimation Transfer Paper on Black Print Quality," *Tekstil ve Konfeksiyon*, vol. 33, no. 4, pp. 366–374, Dec. 2023, doi: 10.32710/tekstilvekonfeksiyon.1145260.
5. D. J. Chen, F. P. Chiang, Y. S. Tan, and H. S. Don, "Digital speckle-displacement measurement using a complex spectrum method," 1993.
6. J. Blaber, B. Adair, and A. Antoniou, "Ncorr: Open-Source 2D Digital Image Correlation Matlab Software," *Exp Mech*, vol. 55, no. 6, pp. 1105–1122, Jul. 2015, doi: 10.1007/s11340-015-0009-1.
7. L. Keene, "A Range and Performance Optimized Version of the Computer-Aided Speckle Interferometry Algorithm for Real-Time Displacement-Strain Field Monitoring," *Exp Tech*, vol. 46, no. 6, pp. 1027–1048, Oct. 2022, doi: 10.1007/s40799-021-00520-x.
8. The MathWords Inc, "Uniformly Distributed Random Numbers," mathworks.com. Accessed: Feb. 17, 2024. [Online]. Available: https://www.mathworks.com/help/matlab/ref/rand.html.
9. J. W. Goodman and Society of Photo-Optical Instrumentation Engineers, *Speckle phenomena in optics: theory and applications*.
10. N. Yusim, A. Giordano, and F. P. Chiang (2024) An Additively Manufactured Pattern Generation Technique for Deformation Analysis of Additively Manufactured Specimens. Advancement of Optical Methods in Experimental Mechanics, 2024 Annual Conference of the Society for Experimental Mechanics; 2024 June 3-6; Vancouver, WA.
11. S. Ri, M. Fujigaki, and Y. Morimoto, "Sampling Moiré Method for Accurate Small Deformation Distribution Measurement," Exp Mech, vol. 50, no. 4, pp. 501–508, Apr. 2010, doi: 10.1007/s11340-009-9239-4.

Chapter 6
Deformation Measurement of Structure Using Sampling Moire Method with SfM-MVS

Shohei Itakura and Motoharu Fujigaki

Abstract SfM-MVS (Structure-from-Motion/Multi-View Stereo) is user-friendly and capable of producing high-quality 3D models without the need for specialized equipment. These advantages are particularly beneficial in the field of measurement. In this study, we proposed a method for deformation measurement of structures using the sampling moire method combined with SfM-MVS. We conducted an experiment using a rubber square beam with a 2D-grating pattern. During the experiment, a weight was placed on the rubber square beam, and 3D models were created both before and after deformation. The displacement distributions obtained using this method were then compared with the value obtained by laser displacement meter. It was confirmed that obstacles were removed through editing, allowing for effective deformation measurement.

Keywords SfM-MVS · Sampling moire method · Displacement measurement · Deformation measurement

Introduction

Recent years, infrastructures such as bridges and tunnels built during the period of high economic growth have been getting dilapidated. They must undergo inspections and maintenance to ensure their longer safety. One of the way to inspect them, Sampling moire method has been proposed and the displacement distributions are obtained using a camera and a 2D-grating [1]. The method has been applied to measure several railroad bridges for high-speed railway. However, in actual sites, there may be cases where obstacles are present in front of the target or where front-facing images cannot be captured due to the target being at a high elevation. Therefore, this study proposes a method for measuring the deformation of target objects by applying the sampling moiré method in a virtual space based on a 3D model created using SfM-MVS. This method enables us to measure objects in that environment because of editing of a 3D model. Using images generated from the 3D model, the feasibility of performing measurements using this method is experimentally investigated.

Proposed Method

SfM-MVS is a technique that generates 3D models from multiple images taken of a target object. This technology is used in various fields such as architecture, civil engineering, and disaster sites, and research on its application in measurement is actively being conducted [2, 3]. The sampling moiré method measures minute displacements by analyzing moiré fringes obtained through image processing of images capturing grid patterns before and after deformation. The proposed method applies the sampling moiré method to obtain displacement distributions by generating images with matching camera positions for the 3D models reconstructed before and after deformation using SfM-MVS. As shown in Figure 1, obstacles can be removed through editing, enabling the generation of images that would otherwise be impossible to capture in reality. At this time, it is essential that the 3D models before and after deformation are placed at the same coordinates in the virtual space, for example, by setting appropriate reference points. Any misalignment in position would appear as displacement in the measurement results; hence, precise alignment is required.

Shohei Itakura · Motoharu Fujigaki
Department of Human and Artificial Intelligent Systems, Graduate School of Engineering, University of Fukui, Bunkyo 3-9-1, Fukui, 910-8507
e-mail: fujigaki@u-fukui.ac.jp

Chi-Hung Hwang et al. (eds.), *Advancement of Optical Methods & Digital Image Correlation in Experimental Mechanics, Vol. 2*, Conference Proceedings
of the Society for Experimental Mechanics Series, https://doi.org/10.13052/9788743808282-6

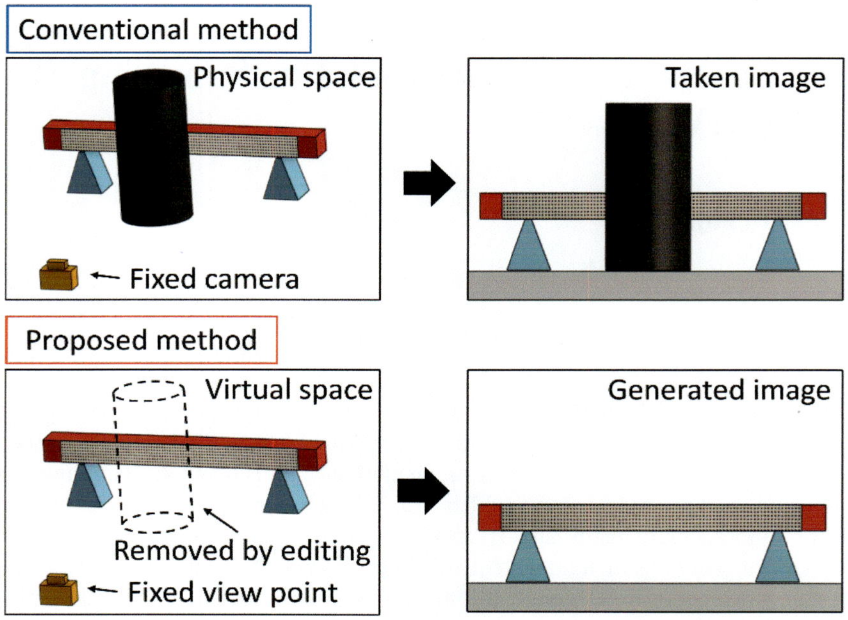

Fig. 1 Conventional method and Proposed method

Experiment

The material used for deformation is a rubber rectangular prism (30 × 60 × 500 mm, hereafter referred to as the beam). A 2D grating with a 4 mm pitch, used for the sampling moiré method, is attached to the side surface of the beam. As shown in Figure 2, an obstacle (PVC pipe) is placed in front of the beam, and a laser displacement meter is positioned so that its pointer hits the center of the object from below.

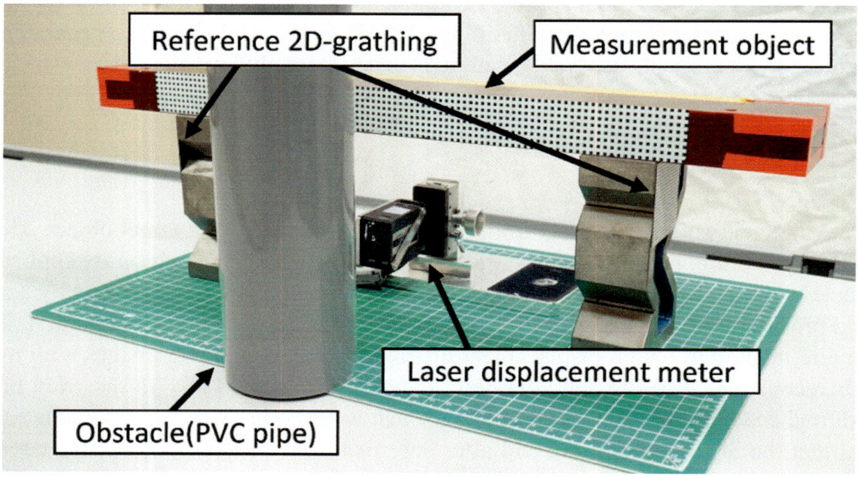

Fig. 2 Experimental environment

3D models of the object are created before and after deformation by placing a weight on the beam. After removing the obstacle from the models through editing, images generated from the same viewpoint are analyzed using the sampling moiré method to measure displacement. Simultaneously, the displacement at the center of the object is measured using the laser displacement meter.

Equipment and Software

The 3D models are created using *iTwin Capture Modeler Master* by Bentley Systems. For visualization, the free software *CloudCompare* is used. *iTwin Capture Modeler* allows users to set the coordinates of any point from the images captured during the 3D modeling process. Additionally, the scale of the models can be adjusted by selecting two points and setting the length of the line segment between them. *CloudCompare* enables the editing of 3D models, fixing viewpoints, and displaying multiple 3D datasets simultaneously within the same coordinate system. The displacement distribution obtained by the sampling moiré method is analyzed using *Fukuface*, a general-purpose image analysis software developed in our laboratory. A *SONY α7S* camera was used, capturing approximately 150 images before and after deformation.

3D Model Alignment

The alignment of the 3D models was performed using the feature for setting reference points from the captured images. As shown in Figure 2, reference grids were placed at both ends of the support structure. The fine patterns of the grid facilitate accurate plotting of reference points, and the precisely determined pitch aids in scale adjustment. As shown in Figure 3, the origin was set on the reference grid, and three additional points were designated as references for the axes and scaling.

Fig. 3 Origin and axis arrangement

Displacement Analysis Results

Figure 4 and 5 show images generated from the 3D models before and after deformation, respectively. The obstacle in front of the target object was removed through editing, and front-facing images of the grid were generated.

Figure 6 (a) and 6 (b) present the displacement distributions in the x and y directions, respectively, obtained by applying the sampling moire method to the edited images in Figure 4 and 5.

The x-direction displacement shows a distribution where both ends appear to lift, while the y-direction displacement shows a distribution where the central portion sinks significantly. These distributions align with the expected displacement patterns when a weight is placed at the center of the object.

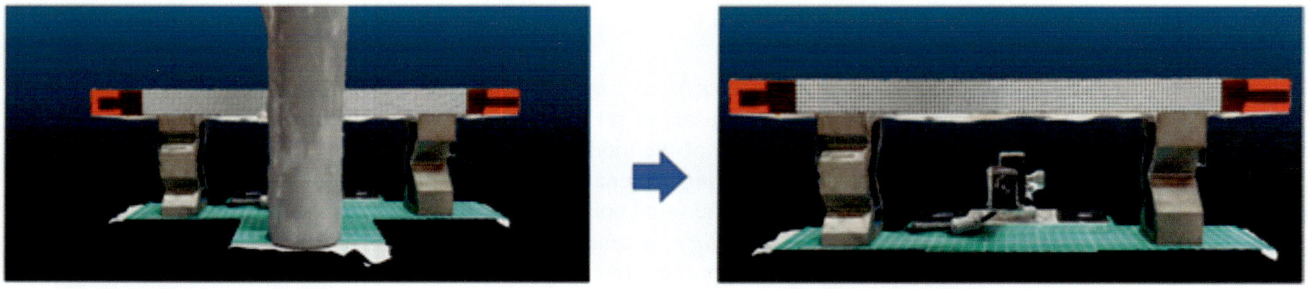

Fig. 4 Images generated from the 3D model before deformation (Left: Before editing, Right: After editing)

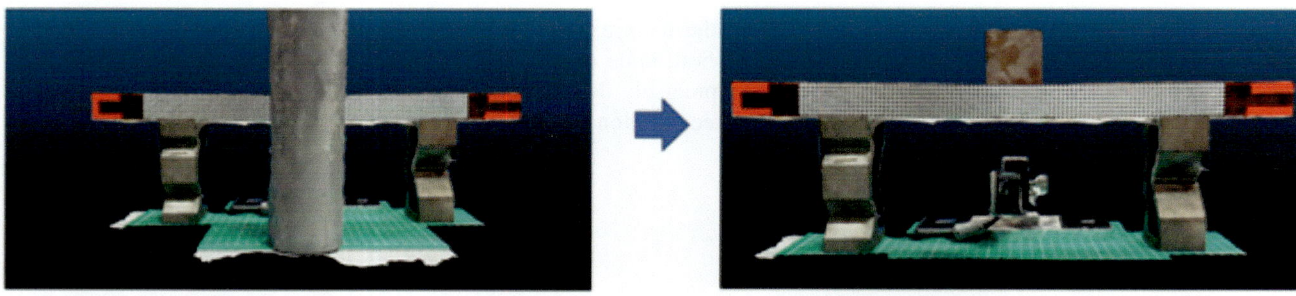

Fig. 5 Images generated from the 3D model after deformation (Left: Before editing, Right: After editing)

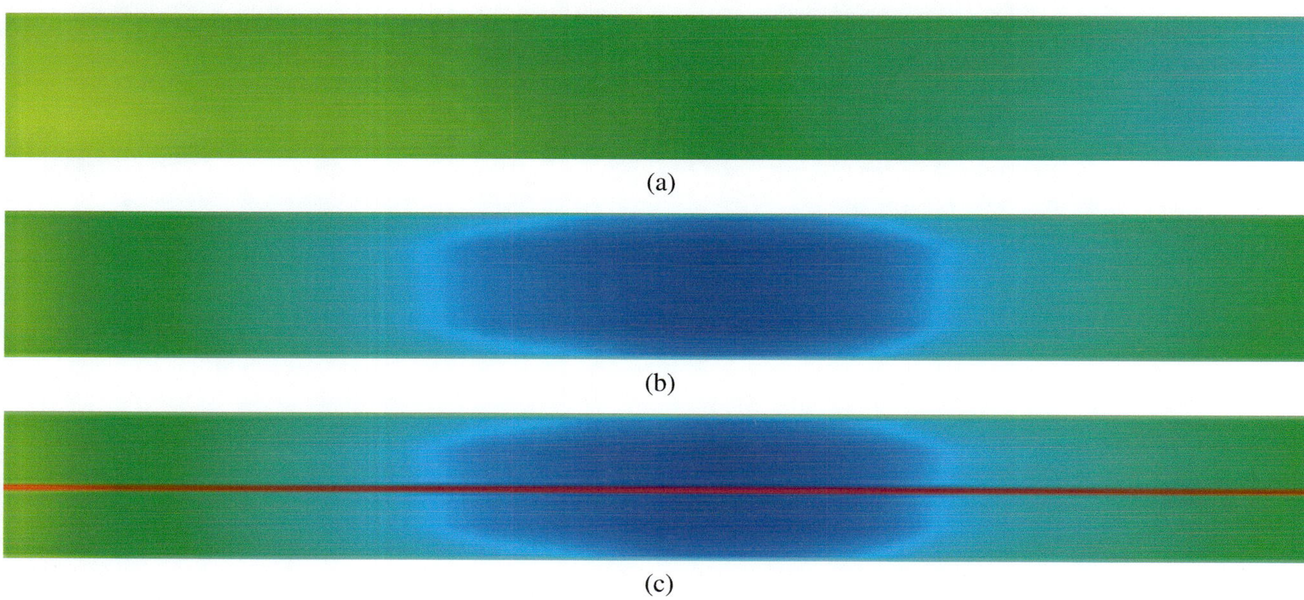

Fig. 6 Displacement Distributions (a) Displacement in the x-direction (b) Displacement in the y-direction (c) Cross-sectional view

Figure 7 shows a graph representing the cross-sectional data along the red line in Figure 6 (c). The displacement at the center of the object is measured as -1.013 mm. The corresponding measurement by the laser displacement meter at the same location is -0.961 mm, resulting in a difference of 0.05 mm.

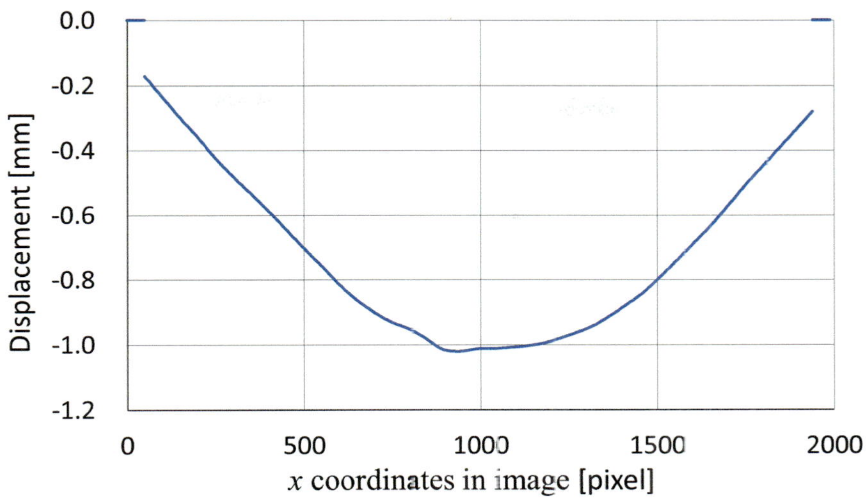

Fig. 7 Cross-sectional Analysis

Conclusion

This paper proposes a method for measuring the deformation of an object by applying the sampling moiré method in a virtual space based on 3D models created using the SfM-MVS technique. The feasibility of this measurement approach was experimentally verified. The proposed approach, which involves generating 3D models before and after deformation in a virtual space and using them to measure displacement distributions, was introduced in this study. To further validate this method, future experiments will be conducted with an expanded range of measurement targets. Ultimately, the goal is to apply this technique to the inspection of infrastructure using drones.

References

1. Ri, S., Fujigaki, M. and Morimoto, Y. "Sampling Moire Method for Accurate Small Deformation Distribution Measurement" *Experimental Mechanics*, April 2010
2. Fuse, T. "Structure from Motion (SfM) Part 2: SfM and Multi-View Stereo" *Photogrammetry and Remote Sensing*, 2016
3. Kanai, S., Date, H., and Tanaka, M. "Generation of 3D Models of Infrastructure Structures Based on Measurements and Their Application to Maintenance and Management" *Measurement and Control*, November 2021

Chapter 7
Development of an *in-situ* Sensor for Real-time Geometrical Inspection in Additive Manufacturing

Howard Zheng, Anthony Salerni and Cosme Furlong

Abstract Real-time measurements in additive manufacturing (AM) are essential for quality control, enabling the early defect detection in critical parameters such as surface contours, subsurface features, and in certain cases the presence of contaminants. Without real-time monitoring, manufacturing inconsistencies, including shape irregularities and chemical impurities, can compromise part quality leading to part failure and waste. To address this challenge, this paper presents the development of a miniaturized, non-contact, full-field surface sensor for real-time AM monitoring *in-situ*. The development follows a two-stage process: first, a testing platform is designed to replicate high-performance AM fabrication conditions, and second, design constraints are identified to establish integration specifications. The sensor employs a structured light projection system using parallel fringes with a stereo-camera setup, utilizing a phase-to-height look-up table to achieve near-video framerate shape recovery. Performance evaluation using USAF targets and NIST-traceable gauges demonstrates spatial and measuring resolutions of 60 μm and 50 μm, respectively, validating its capability for defect detection and quality control. During operation, the sensor continuously acquires surface geometry data for each printed layer, enabling the creation of a high-resolution digital representation of the AM part. Future efforts will focus on integrating machine learning algorithms for automated compensation, further enhancing fabrication accuracy and process efficiency.

Keywords Additive manufacturing · Fringe projection · *In-situ* measurements · Sensor miniaturization · Smart manufacturing

Introduction

In the evolving landscape of manufacturing, accurate and reliable fabrication processes are essential. Recent advancements in additive manufacturing (AM) have enabled the production of components with complex geometries and higher tolerances, spurring interest in the development of real-time, *in-situ* sensors with a range of measurement modalities. Beyond surface contours, such sensors can capture subsurface defects and monitor chemical impurities in real-time, ensuring comprehensive quality assessments throughout the fabrication process. These wide-ranging measurement capabilities are crucial for maintaining part integrity and optimizing quality control across the entire fabrication processes of AM components. By detecting irregularities at an early stage, *in-situ* monitoring can significantly reduce material waste, improve production efficiency, and enhance the overall reliability of AM-produced parts.

Traditional *ex-situ* inspection methods, such as coordinate-measuring machines and ultrasonic inspection, provide precise measurements of the surface and subsurface features, but only after fabrication is completed. This post-process evaluation results in delayed defect detection, increased production costs, and limited opportunities for corrective actions. In contrast, *in-situ* inspection offers real-time monitoring, enabling early identification of anomalies, and generates an evolving digital representation of the AM part during fabrication. However, designing a miniaturized, non-invasive *in-situ* sensor comes with technical challenges, including achieving high spatial and temporal resolutions, avoiding interference with the AM processes, and ensuring compatibility with various printing environments. Furthermore, the integration of data mining techniques and machine-learning (ML) algorithms enhances the potential of *in-situ* sensing by enabling the use of quantitative

Howard Zheng · Anthony Salerni · Cosme Furlong
Center for Holographic Studies and Laser micro-mechaTronics (CHSLT), Mechanical & Materials Engineering Department, Worcester Polytechnic Institute, Worcester, MA 01609
e-mail: hzheng3@wpi.edu; asalerni72@wpi.edu; cfurlong@wpi.edu

Chi-Hung Hwang et al. (eds.), *Advancement of Optical Methods & Digital Image Correlation in Experimental Mechanics, Vol. 2*, Conference Proceedings
of the Society for Experimental Mechanics Series, https://doi.org/10.13052/9788743808282-7

measurements to dynamically optimize fabrication parameters. For instance, ML-based systems can automatically adjust print speed, bed temperature, and extrusion rate to compensate for detected irregularities, paving the way for intelligent, adaptive manufacturing processes.

This paper focuses on surface shape measurements and presents progress in assembling a testing platform that replicates AM printing conditions and identifying design constraints that establish integration specifications. Preliminary results, including real-time measurements stitching, are presented, as well as the spatial and temporal resolutions achieved.

Methodology

To properly evaluate the performance of the surface shape sensor, a testing platform is first assembled. This testing platform is designed to replicate AM printing conditions similar to those of a high-performance AM system. The specifications of the testing platform are determined based on the parameters of the targeted AM system, such as the resolution and travelling speed in *x, y,* and *z* axes. Other key optical design (e.g., working distance, illumination wavelength, and field-of-view) are also defined by the constraints of the AM system. The testing platform also incorporates replicas of key structures from the AM system. This allows the sensor's fixtures to be designed around these structures for seamless integration into the AM environment with minimal obstruction to the printing process.

Based on the design constraints identified through construction of the testing platform, a non-invasive, miniaturized surface shape sensor are designed. A structured light fringe projection (FP) system with parallel fringes is employed for surface shape reconstruction. Major components of the FP system include an object of interest, a projector for fringe projection, and a camera to capture the distorted fringe pattern. The three components form a triangulation geometry as shown in Figure 1, and the full field depth information can be recovered via the phase-to-height relationship [1], given by equation

$$\overline{MM'} = \frac{L\Omega}{2\pi f_o D}, \tag{1}$$

where $\overline{MM'}$ is the height of the object at position (*x,y*), L is the distance from the projector's pupil to a reference plane, D is the distance from the projector's pupil to the camera's pupil, f_o is the spatial frequency of the projected fringes, and Ω is

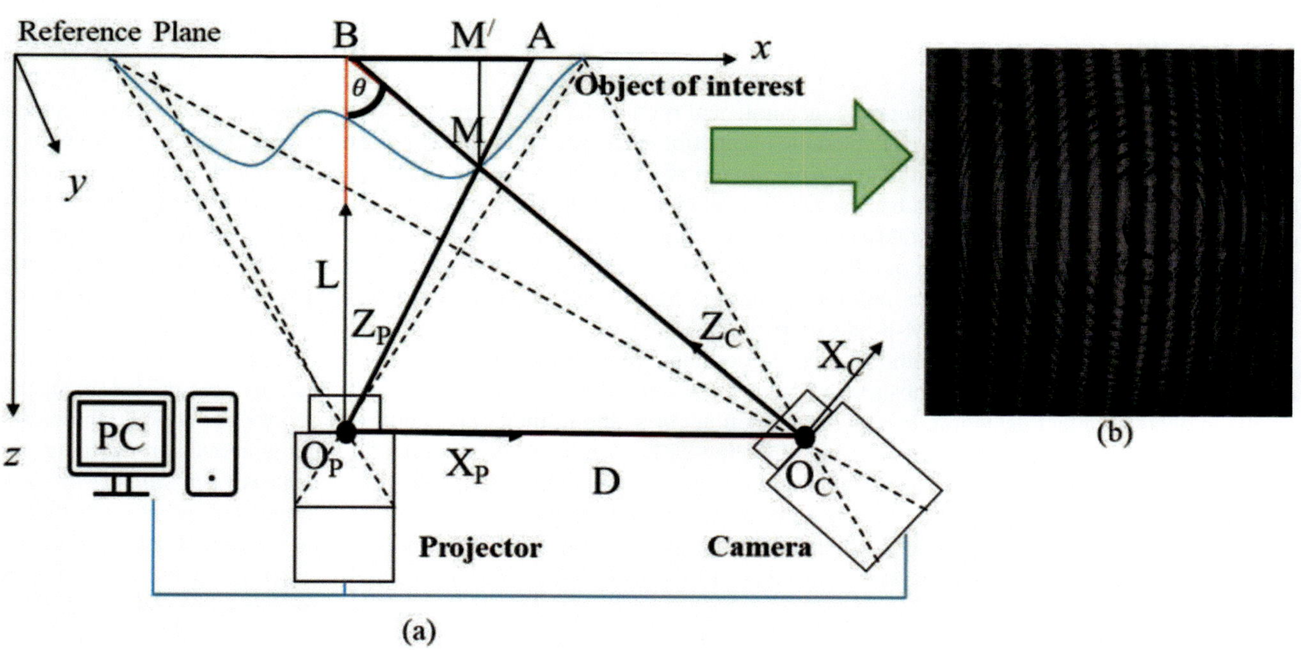

Fig. 1 Fringe projection methodology setup using triangulation principle: (a) schematic of fringe projection system showing the triangulation geometry of the object, projector, and camera; and (b) representative fringe projection pattern on an object of interest.

the optical phase carrying the shape information. The optical phase, Ω, can be extracted via phase-stepping, Fourier domain analysis, or sampling Moiré method [2–5]. However, due to the nature of phase calculation using inverse tangent function, the phase map may contain 2π discontinuities that must be unwrapped before depth can be computed. Phase unwrapping can be done using various methods, including temporal phase unwrapping, quality-guided phase unwrapping, and direct phase-to-height look-up tables [6–8]. For the proposed miniaturized sensor, the direct phase-to-height technique is used because it offers significantly faster computation than the other methods [9].

Realization of Testing Platform and Surface Sensor

Testing platform

Realization of the dynamic testing platform begins with matching both the dynamic and structural criteria of the intended AM system. Dynamic criteria involve matching the fabrication speed and acceleration of the AM system, as well as its movement resolutions along each axis. Structural criteria require the testing platform to have an identical print-head fixture to establish design constraints for seamless integration of the surface sensor. Figure 2 shows a representative FDM-type AM printer, and the realized testing platform constructed around these dynamic and structural criteria. To satisfy the dynamic requirements, the testing platform employs motorized *x-y* stages that can reach speed up to 200 mm/s with a resolution of 2.5 μm. The platform must also be controllable via G-code, similar to a standard AM system. Structurally, the platform provides a fixture to attach the surface sensor such that the sensor does not interfere with the printing process. A mock print nozzle is attached to the platform to simulate the obstacle presented by an actual AM print-head.

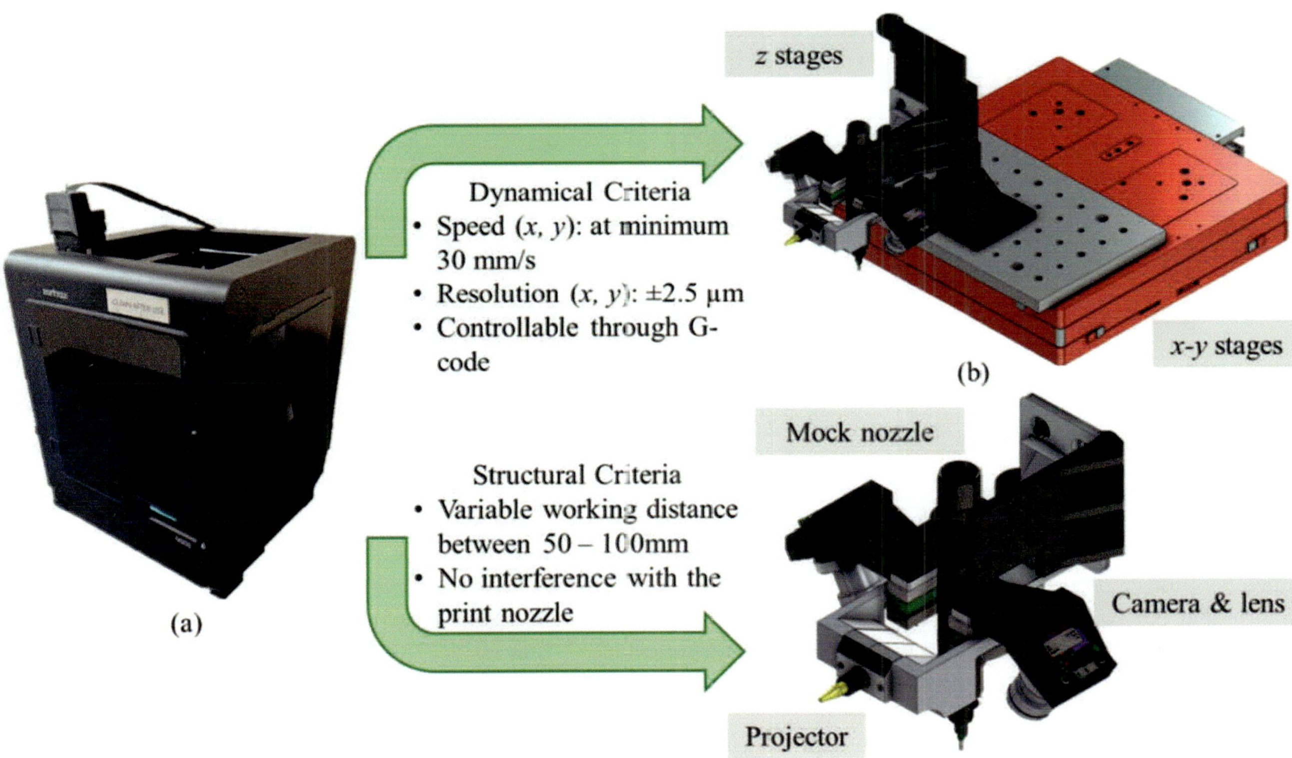

Fig. 2 Schematic illustrating the realization of testing platform by matching the AM system's dynamic and structural criteria: (a) representative FDM-type AM system; (b) testing platform with high-speed, high-precision motorized stages; and (c) replicated print-head with added imaging optics, projectors, and a mocked print nozzle to simulate obstacle in actual AM processes.

Real-time in-situ surface sensor

One major obstacle in applying FP setup for real-time AM measurement is the interference from the printing nozzle. In a conventional FP arrangement, the projector would occupy the same position as the printing nozzle, an obvious conflict. Therefore, the projection path needs to be redirected and rescaled from a different angle to avoid collision with the nozzle. Figure 3 shows the optical design and implementation of such an off-axis projection system. The illumination is introduced from a direction perpendicular to the nozzle, and a biconic mirror together with a biconcave lens are used to redirect and rescale the fringe projection to the appropriate size on the reference plane.

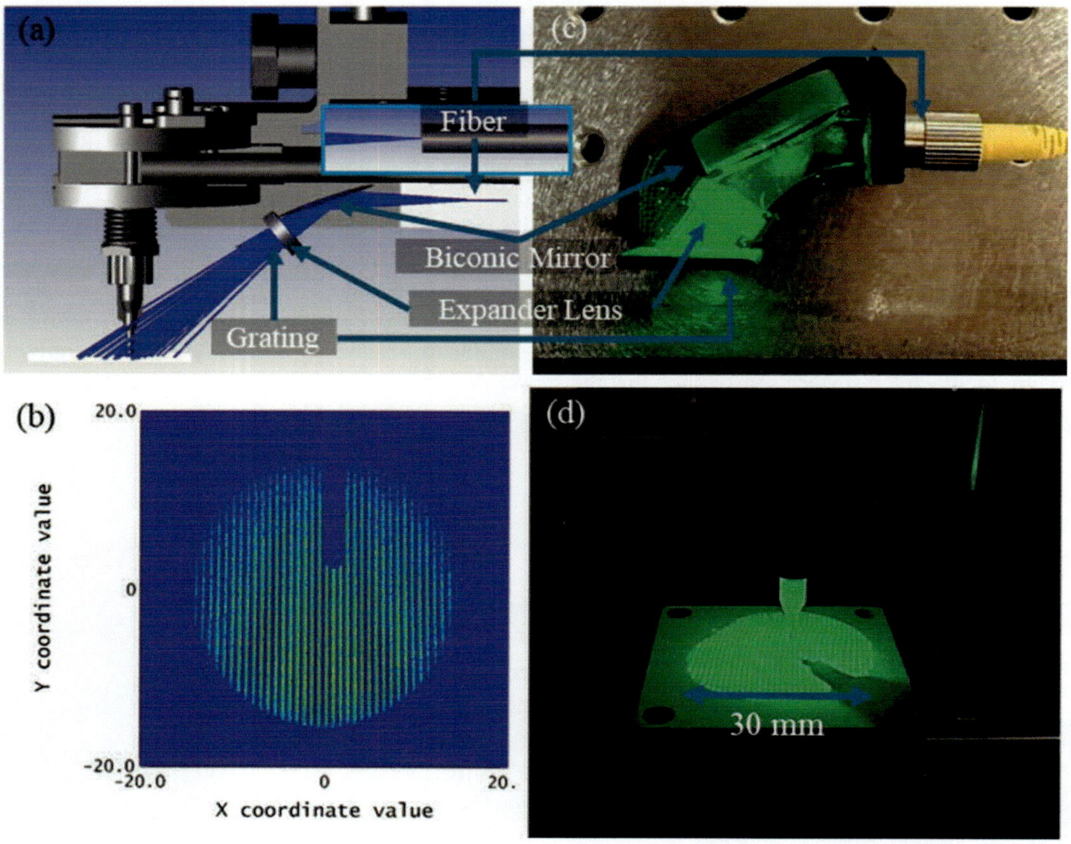

Fig. 3 Design and implementation of the off-axis fringe projection system using a biconic mirror and biconcave expander lens: (a) optical design (Zemax simulation) to obtain the parameters required to redirect and rescale the fringes at the reference plane; (b) simulated projection output accounting for the shadowing effect of the nozzle; (c) physical realization of the off-axis fringe projection system; and (d) implementation of the system shown in (c).

To miniaturize the overall sensor setup, board-level cameras with low profile lens are used. Table 1 provides key parameters of the camera and lens used in the observation system. The selected board-level cameras included general purpose input/output (GPIO) channels that can be configured for stroboscopic imaging, thereby reducing motion blur that would otherwise introduced noise during real-time surface measurements.

Table 1 A list of the camera and lens used in the observation system with relevant parameters

Camera	Lens
Basler daA1920-160um	M12-threaded Lens
2.3 MP full resolution	50° FOV
160 frames per second maximum	6 mm focal length
$30 \times 30 \times 20$ mm^3	$16 \times 16 \times 10$ mm^3
15 grams	7 grams

Representative 3D Reconstruction and Stitching

The spatial and measuring capabilities of the surface sensor are validated using a USAF target and a custom-made NIST traceable target. Figure 4 shows the NIST traceable target and its sinusoidal surface profile design. The sinusoidal NIST target is designed to have a peak-to-peak depth of 0.5 mm and a period of 5 mm; these parameters are chosen based on the project sponsor requirements. Figure 5 shows an image of the USAF target captured with the Basler daA1920-160um camera using the 50° FOV lens at a working distance of 100 mm, and the corresponding 3D reconstruction of the sinusoidal NIST traceable target. The characterized spatial (x, y) resolution is approximately 62.5 μm and the measuring (z) resolution is approximately 50 μm. Figure 6 illustrates a representative surface measurement stitching result with the sensor operating in real time under a 120 mm/s motion of the testing platform. In figure 6, panels (a)-(d) shows small-area surface measurements at four different time instances, each outlined in a different color; panel (e) shows the stitched single-layer measurements, with outlines corresponding to the colored areas from (a)-(d).

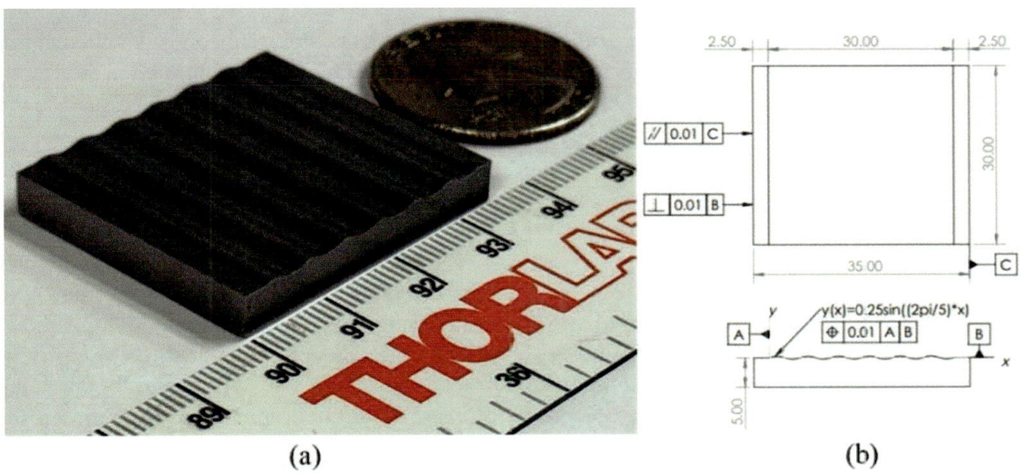

Fig. 4 NIST traceable target used to validate the sensor's measuring resolution: (a) image of the NIST traceable target with the designed sinusoidal surface profile; and (b) design drawing of the NIST traceable target, where the sinusoidal surface profile is defined by $y(x) = 0.25\sin(0.4\pi x)$.

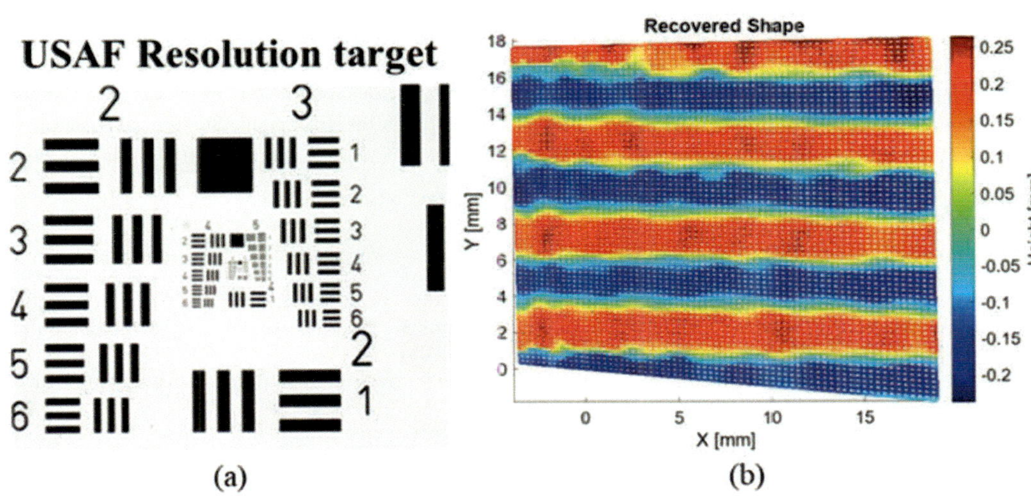

Fig. 5 Spatial and measuring resolution of the surface sensor: (a) image of a USAF target taken with the Basler daA1920-160um camera (50° FOV lens, 100 mm working distance); and (b) 3D reconstruction of the sinusoidal NIST traceable target. The spatial and measuring resolutions are approximately 62.5 μm and 50 μm, respectively.

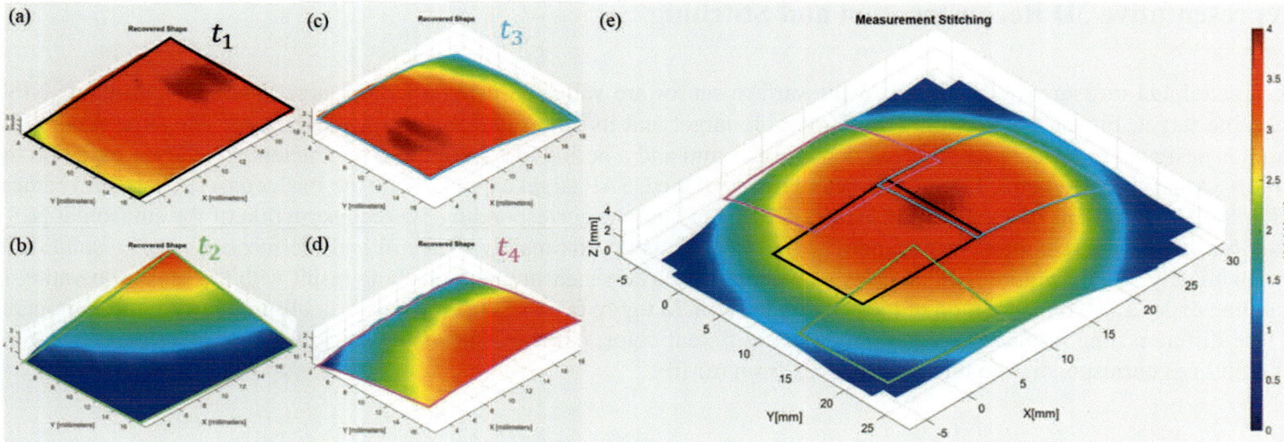

Fig. 6 Representative surface measurements taken at different time instances while the senor is subjected to 120 mm/s motion: (a)-(d) show small area surface measurements at four different time instances, each outlined in a different color; and (e) shows the stitched single-layer measurement, with colored outlines corresponding to the small area surface measurements in (a)-(d).

Conclusion and Future Works

The current results demonstrate the feasibility of the assembled testing platform in matching the actual AM processing parameters both dynamically and structurally. The miniaturized surface sensor utilizing FP methodology shows promising preliminary results in capturing depth information in motion and in real time. The single-layer stitching result indicates that the sensor is suitable for monitoring an AM part *in-situ*, during fabrication: as the part is built layer by layer, the sensor can record the depth information at each layer, ultimately forming a complete 3D digital representation of the finished part.

Future works will focus on improving the spatial and measuring resolution through advance filtering method and optimization of the observation and projection systems. Additional efforts will be placed on investigating composite shape recovery methods to augment the phase-to-height look-up table, since the look-up table method suffers from a limited measurements range [10]. By adding a coarse height estimation step before the look-up table, the effective measurement range can be increased significantly. Overall, the current developments serve as a starting point for optimizing a real-time surface sensor for *in-situ* AM applications and can be tailored to specific types of AM environments. It is envisioned that additional measurement capabilities, such as subsurface sensing and chemical analysis, can be integrated into the current sensor in the future to create a comprehensive and multimodal real-time, *in-situ* AM monitoring system.

Acknowledgments We sincerely acknowledge the Department of Energy for their generous sponsorship, which has been instrumental in the success of this project. Additionally, we extend our gratitude to our colleagues at the Center for Holographic Studies and Laser micro-mechaTronics (CHSLT) for their invaluable support and assistance throughout the research.

References

1. Chen, X., Xi, J.,Tao, J. and Ye, J., "Research and development of an accurate 3D shape measurement system based on fringe projection: Model analysis and performance evaluation," *Prec. Engg., 32*, pp. 215-221, 2008.
2. Ruiz-Cadalso, D. and Furlong, C., "Application of instantaneous polarization imagers for quantitative optical metrology by digital holography," *Proc., SEM 2024 Annu. Conf.*, 2024.
3. Takeda, M. and Mutoh, K., "Fourier transform profilometry for the automatic measurement of 3-d object shapes," *Appl. Opt.*, *22*(24), pp.3977-3982, 1983.
4. Huang, L., Qian, K., Pan, B. and Asundi, A., "Comparison of Fourier transform, windowed Fourier transform, and wavelet transform methods for phase extraction from a single fringe pattern in fringe projection profilometry," *Opt. Lasers Engg.*, *48*(2), pp. 141–148, 2010.
5. Ri. S., Fujigaki, M. and Morimoto, Y., "Sampling Moiré method for accurate small deformation distribution measurement," *Exp Mech*, *50*(4), pp. 501–508, 2010.
6. Zou, C., Huang, L., Zhang, M., Chen, Q. and Asundi, A., "Temporal phase unwrapping algorithms for fringe projection profilometry: A comparative review," *Opt. Lasers in Eng.*, *85*, pp. 84–103, 2016.

7. Zhao, M., Huang, L., Zhang, Q., Su, X., Asundi, A. and Kemao, Q., "Quality-guided phase unwrapping technique: comparison of quality maps and guiding strategies," *Appl. Opt., 50*(33), p. 6214, 2011.
8. Suzuki, S., Akatsuka, Y., Jiang, W., Fujigaki, M. and Otsu, M., "Development of quick three-dimensional shape measurement projection mapping system using a whole-space tabulation method," *Appl. Sci., 9*(20), p. 4408, 2019.
9. Zheng, H., Salerni, A. and Furlong, C., "Real-time surface metrology in-situ by dual-frequency fringe projection to augment smart manufacturing," *Proc., SEM 2024 Annu. Conf.*, 2024.
10. Guo, W., Wu, Z., Xu, R., Zhang, Q., and Fujigaki, M., "A fast reconstruction method for three-dimensional shape measurement using dual-frequency grating projection and phase-to-height lookup table." *Opt. Laser Technol., 112*, pp.269–277, 2019.

Chapter 8
Development of Mixed Reality Methods for Immersive Visualization of 3D Dynamic Optical Testing Measurements

Daniel Ruiz-Cadalso, Lorena Maria Genua, Jonathan Oliveira Luiz, Cosme Furlong, Lee Moradi, and Vladimir Vantsevich

Abstract Conventional techniques for visualization of optical experimental data, such as displacements and vibrations, as well as numerical simulations remain limited to 2D screens, lacking the opportunity for more intuitive spatial analysis. In this work, we are developing a methodology that explores the use of MR to overlay experimental optical measurement data directly onto the physical objects under analysis. Digital fringe projection and holographic interferometry techniques are applied to shape and vibration measurements, respectively, of real aerospace rotor blades subjected to dynamic loading conditions. The high-resolution, full-field displacement data is processed, applied to the shape measurement, and visualized in an MR environment using Microsoft HoloLens2 by a custom-developed application running on Unity, enabling users to directly interact with 3D data. This initial methodology demonstrates the potential of merging experimental data with numerical simulations for real-time investigation of actual components and facilitating the development of digital twins.

Keywords Mixed reality · Digital holography · Digital twins · Optical metrology · Non-destructive testing.

Introduction

Optical metrology is critical for non-destructive testing (NDT) in experimental mechanics, enabling precise, full-field measurement of displacement, strain, and vibration in a variety of engineering and biological applications. Techniques such as digital holographic interferometry, digital image correlation (DIC), structured light projection, and digital shearography offer non-contact, high-resolution measurements, and have been employed in a variety of applications [1], from NDT in the aerospace industry [2–4] to structural health monitoring, and biomedical imaging. Traditional visualization of data collected from these methods is often limited to two-dimensional (2D) representations on standard display screens, hampering a more intuitive spatial understanding of complex, dynamic data.

To address these limitations, mixed reality (MR) and digital twin technologies are being explored to enhance the way optical metrology data is analyzed and interpreted. By overlaying experimental data onto physical samples in a 3D interactive

Daniel Ruiz-Cadalso · Jonathan Oliveira Luiz · Cosme Furlong
Center for Holographic Studies and Laser micro-mechaTronics (CHSLT)
e-mail: daruizcadalso@wpi.edu; joluiz@wpi.edu; cfurlong@wpi.edu

Cosme Furlong · Lee Moradi · Vladimir Vantsevich
Autonomous Vehicle Mobility Institute (AVMI)
e-mail: cfurlong@wpi.edu; lmoradi@wpi.edu; vvantsevich@wpi.edu

Daniel Ruiz-Cadalso · Jonathan Oliveira Luiz · Cosme Furlong · Lee Moradi · Vladimir Vantsevich
Mechanical & Materials Engineering Department
e-mail: daruizcadalso@wpi.edu; joluiz@wpi.edu; cfurlong@wpi.edu; lmoradi@wpi.edu; vvantsevich@wpi.edu

Lorena Maria Genua
Robotics Engineering Department, Worcester Polytechnic Institute, Worcester, MA
e-mail: lgenua@wpi.edu

Chi-Hung Hwang et al. (eds.), *Advancement of Optical Methods & Digital Image Correlation in Experimental Mechanics, Vol. 2*, Conference Proceedings
of the Society for Experimental Mechanics Series, https://doi.org/10.13052/9788743808282-8

environment, users can intuitively explore and manipulate datasets in real-time. Prior work has demonstrated the use of augmented reality (AR) for visualizing holographic data obtained through DH [5]. Other studies have employed MR for ultrasonics imaging, where dynamics extracted from experimental data are directly overlaid on structures for real-time evaluation [6]. Digital twins in optical metrology are particularly useful in applications where real-time experimental feedback is used to update numerical models for better predictive capabilities [7, 8].

In this study, we propose a methodology that integrates mixed reality visualization with optical metrology techniques, specifically structured light projection and digital holographic interferometry. Our approach enables direct overlay of high-resolution experimental data and numerical simulations onto physical objects for real-time evaluation. The integration of MR tools allows users to interact with 3D full-field shape and displacement data, enhancing the interpretation of experimental and numerical results.

Materials and Methods

Mixed reality display

For mixed reality visualization, we utilize Microsoft HoloLens 2 [9], an optical see-through head-mounted display that enables real-time interaction with projected data [10]. The experimental optical metrology data can be processed using a custom-developed C# application running within Unity, which serves as the rendering engine for graphical data representation. The application, described in Figure 1, enables users to visualize and manipulate full-field displacement, strain, and vibration data overlaid on real test samples. Through custom Unity shaders and rendering techniques, high-resolution optical metrology data is spatially aligned with the physical object under investigation.

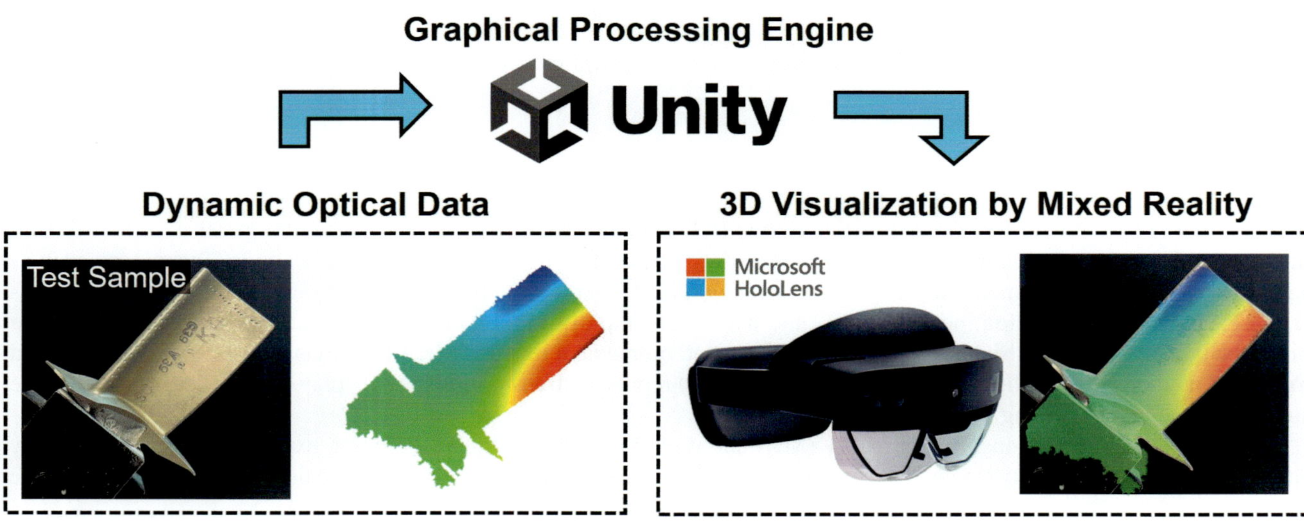

Fig. 1 Implementation of mixed reality tools for 3D visualization of dynamic optical data. The data is processed and imported into the Unity engine, and a custom-developed program runs the engine through the HoloLens 2.

Optical metrology techniques

Digital fringe projection

Structured light projection is a technique for recovering 3D shape information of an object's surface. In fringe projection, a structured fringe pattern with known phase and density is used. Our fringe projection system consists of two major components: a spatial light modulator (SLM) and a digital charged-couple device (CCD) camera. The SLM projects computer generated fringe patterns onto a sample of interest, and the CCD captures the fringe patterns on the sample. The camera is positioned at an angle from the projection axis in order to provide optical triangulation, which describes the sensitivity of the data. Due to optical triangulation, height, h, can be extracted via [11],

$$h = \frac{L\Phi}{2\pi f_0 D}, \tag{1}$$

where h is the height from the reference plane, L is the distance from the SLM to a reference plane, D is the distance from the SLM to the CCD camera, f_0 is the spatial frequency of the projected fringes, and Φ is the optical phase carrying shape information. The optical phase, Φ, is extracted via phase-shifting methods [12].

Digital holographic interferometry

Digital holography is an optical technique used to extract the amplitude and phase of light. In order to properly extract these parameters, digital holography uses the superposition of two unique coherent wavefronts which stem from the same light source but have each undergone diverse conditions in their respective paths. The recorded complex field, $\Gamma = Ae^{i\Phi}$, is reconstructed using phase-shifted holograms, either temporally or spatially [13]. The optical phase calculated from a single reconstructed field would yield static information; thus, changes to the optical phase are measured interferometrically via a double exposure (DE) method. The phase difference values are wrapped within $[-\pi,\ \pi]$ (mod2π). The phase can be unwrapped, and directly converted to displacements, d, by [12],

$$d = \frac{\lambda}{4\pi}\mathrm{unwrap}\left[\Delta\Phi\right], \tag{2}$$

where d is the displacement, λ is the wavelength of the source, and $\mathrm{unwrap}\left[\Delta\Phi\right]$ is the unwrapped optical phase.

Representative Results

Experimental results of optical methods

Shape measurements by structured light fringe projection

The results of structured light projection for shape measurements are shown in Figure 2. The fringe projection system captured the 3D surface profile of the sample with 5 MP spatial resolution and below 100 μm measurement accuracy. As shown in Figures 2a and 2b, the sample was illuminated using a spatial light modulator (SLM), and fringe patterns were captured

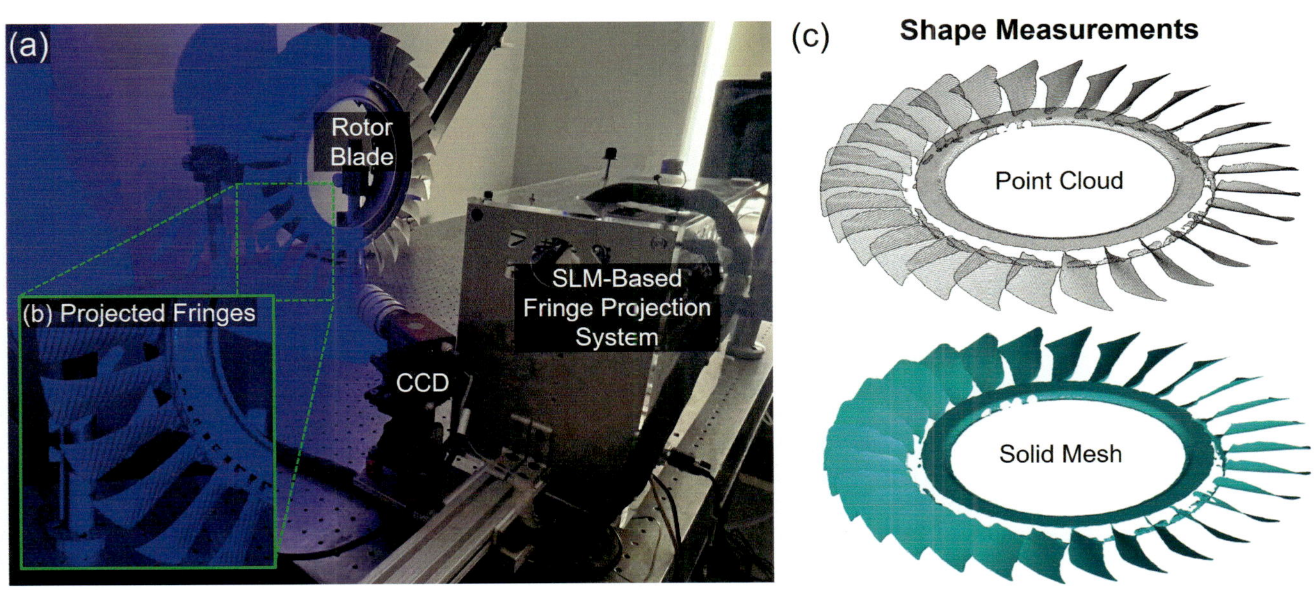

Fig. 2 Shape measurements by digital fringe projection: (a) system setup; (b) zoomed-in image showing the projected 460 nm fringes; and (b) 3D shape results as a point cloud as well as a solid mesh.

by a CCD camera positioned at an offset angle for triangulation-based reconstruction. The quantitative accuracy of shape measurement is assessed based on spatial resolution and phase-unwrapping techniques. Due to nondisclosure agreements, the specific dimensions of the sample cannot be provided, but the system demonstrated a shape measurement resolution in the sub-100 μm range. The extracted 3D mesh, shown in Figure 2c, provides precise surface reconstruction, which can be further analyzed in mixed reality environments for digital twin applications.

Vibration measurements by digital holographic interferometry

The vibrational displacement measurements obtained using digital holographic interferometry (DHI) are illustrated in Figure 3. The setup, shown in Figure 3a, features a custom-developed digital holographic system consisting of a compact and portable optical head, a 532 nm, continuous-wave, single longitudinal mode laser, and a 5 MP camera. The sample was loaded using a piezoelectric shaker attached along the circumference of the rotor's rim, inducing dynamic deformations, which were captured in real-time at 15 fps. The optical phase changes were processed to extract mode shapes and displacement fields down to approximately 26 nm in resolution. The results include displacement fields at a specific mode shape, shown in Figures 3b and 3c.

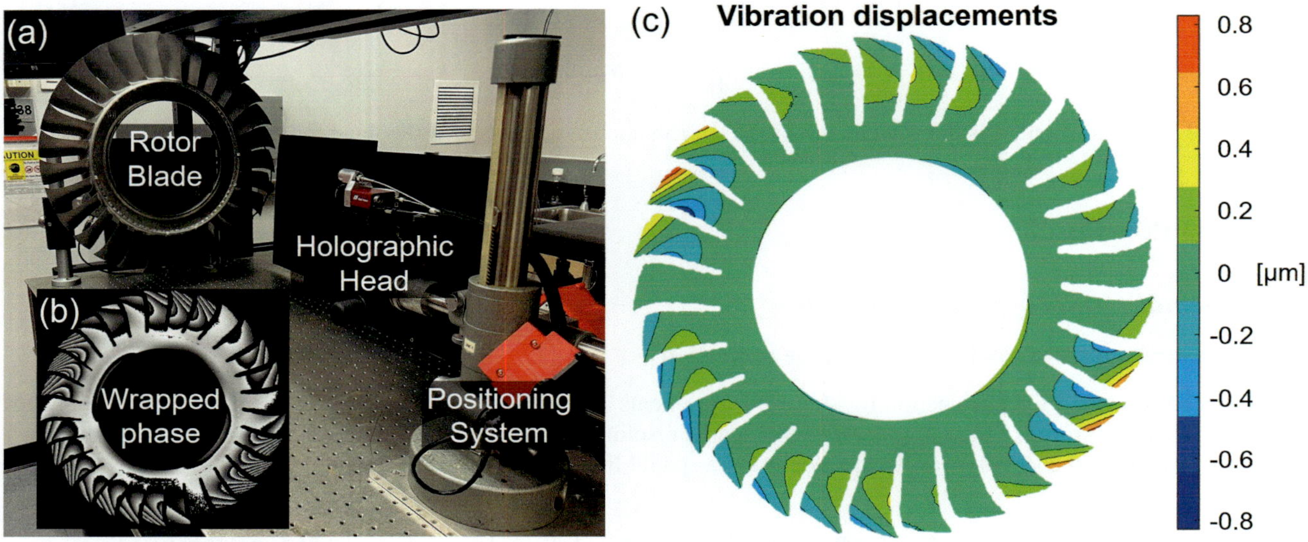

Fig. 3 Vibrational displacement measurements by digital holographic interferometry: (a) system setup; (b) wrapped optical phase of the complete rotor blade; and (c) displacement fields of one mode shape.

Visualization of rotor vibrations by mixed reality

The final experimental demonstration involved using mixed reality visualization to project optical metrology data onto an actual rotor sample, as depicted in Figure 4. Figure 4a shows the 3rd person view of the user interacting with the optical data in real-time. The displacement data obtained from digital holographic interferometry was mapped onto the rotor surface in real-time, as shown in Figures 4b, 4c and 4d, allowing users to interactively examine mode shapes and vibrational characteristics. The data visualization was performed using manual placement within the MR environment, with plans for future automation through image-based registration. The frame rate of the MR display was maintained at 60 Hz, ensuring smooth rendering, with occasional and short dips to 30 Hz, while the accuracy of holographic data alignment was within millimeter precision. Future developments will enhance automatic registration techniques for improved data alignment.

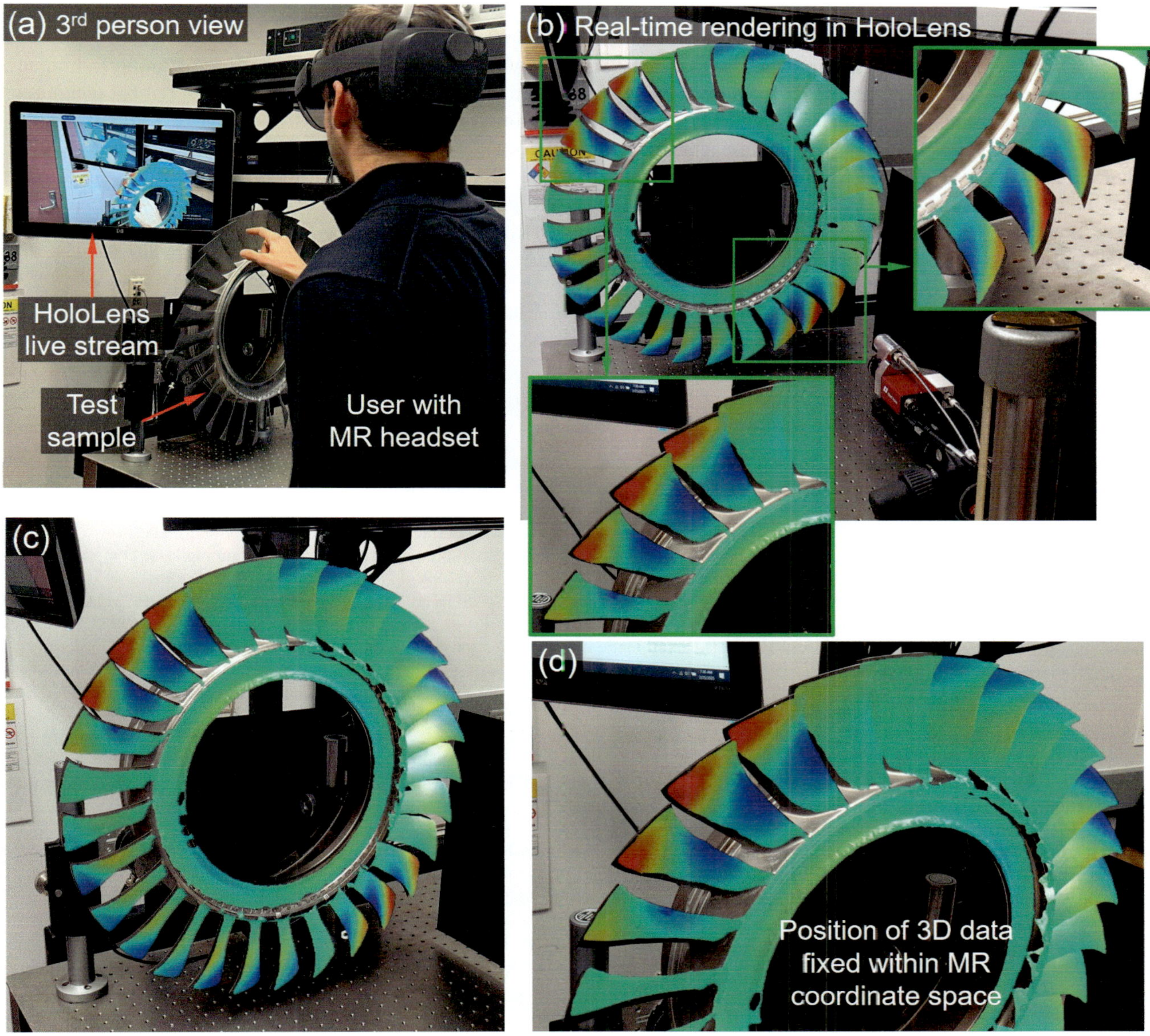

Fig. 4 Augmented visualizations of digital holographic interferometry data by mixed reality methods using HoloLens technology: (a) image of the user from a 3rd person point of view, while displaying the live stream of the HoloLens results using first mode shape; (b) snapshots taken via the HoloLens stream; (c) overlay of entire dynamic optical data on the real sample; and (d) different angle of view.

Conclusions and Future Work

This study demonstrates the integration of mixed reality with optical metrology techniques, including structured light projection, digital holographic interferometry, and high-speed digital image correlation. By leveraging HoloLens 2 and Unity, we successfully visualized full-field 3D experimental data in an interactive MR environment. The results highlight the potential of MR for intuitive interpretation of dynamic optical measurements, offering a more immersive and spatially accurate representation of experimental data compared to conventional 2D visualization methods.

Despite the promising results, several challenges remain in the implementation of MR-based optical metrology visualization. The handling of large datasets poses computational challenges, requiring efficient processing methods to ensure real-time rendering. Additionally, the accurate registration of data with the geometry is crucial for precise alignment of MR overlays with physical samples. Another challenge lies in real-time synchronization, as improvements in frame rate stability and spatial accuracy are necessary for seamless integration and user interaction.

Future work will focus on enhancing the automatic placement of MR data using image and shape registration techniques, which will improve alignment accuracy and reduce manual intervention. The integration of shape measurement techniques with dynamic metrology is another key area of development, enabling a more comprehensive digital twin representation. Additionally, modifying geometry visualization using exaggerated displacement fields can enhance the spatial understanding of the optical data, making it easier to interpret dynamic behaviors. The potential for real-time modal correlation through MR will also be explored, further strengthening the capabilities of digital twins in predictive analysis. Overall, this research lays the foundation for MR-enhanced optical metrology, offering significant advancements for applications in nondestructive evaluation, biomechanics, and structural health monitoring.

Acknowledgments Partial support from multiple sources is acknowledged, including that from our industry sponsors and from the CHSLT and AVMI laboratories at WPI. Contributions by Gabriel de Oliveira are appreciated.

References

1. Ruiz-Cadalso, D. and Furlong, C., "High-resolution imaging for in-situ non-destructive testing by quantitative lensless digital holography," *Frontiers in Photonics*, *5*, 2024.
2. Newman, J.W., "Holographic and shearographic NDT applications in aerospace manufacturing," *Mater. Eval.*, *63*(7), 2005.
3. Ruiz-Cadalso, D. and Furlong, C., "Comparative study of high-speed digital holographic interferometry and scanning laser Doppler vibrometry for modal analysis," *Proc., SEM 2023 Annu. Conf.*, 2023.
4. Ruiz-Cadalso, D. and Furlong, C., "Nondestructive Crack Detection by High-Speed Digital Holographic Interferometry and Impact-Induced Traveling Waves," *Proc., SEM 2023 Annu. Conf.,* 2023.
5. O'Connor, T., Rawat, S., Markman, A. and Javidi, B., "Automatic cell identification and visualization using digital holographic microscopy with head mounted augmented reality devices," *Applied Optics*, *57*(7), 2018.
6. Rehbein, J., Lorenz, S.J., Holtmannspötter, J. and Valeske, B., "3D-visualization of ultrasonic NDT data using mixed reality," *J. Nondestruct. Eval.*, *41*(1), p.26, 2022.
7. Lai, X., Kan, Z., Sun, W., Song, X., Tian, B. and Yuan, T., "Digital twin-based non-destructive testing for structural health monitoring of bridges," *NDT & E, 39*(1), pp.57-74, 2024.
8. Shin, J.H., Park, S.J., Kim, M.A., Lee, M.J., Lim, S.C. and Cho, K.W., "Development of a digital twin pipeline for interactive scientific simulation and mixed reality visualization," *IEEE Access*, *11*, 2023.
9. *Microsoft HoloLens 2*, Microsoft, 2019.
10. Genua, L.M., Boguslavskii, N. and Li, Z., "Multilateral Multimodal Human-Robot Collaboration for Robotic Nursing Assistance: Prototype System and Preliminary User Study," *33rd IEEE RO-MAN 2024*, pp. 1457-1462, 2024.
11. Zheng, H., Salerni, A. and Furlong, C., "Shape Measurements in Additive Manufacturing by Structured Light Projection In Situ," *Proc., SEM 2023 Annu. Conf.*, pp. 59-65, 2023.
12. Kreis, T., *Holographic interferometry: principles and methods*, Wiley-VCH, 1996.
13. Ruiz-Cadalso, D. and Furlong, C., "Application of instantaneous polarization imagers for quantitative optical metrology by digital holography," *Proc., SEM 2024 Annu. Conf.*, 2024.

Chapter 9
Development of an Instantaneous Phase-shifting Lensless Digital Holographic Otoscope for Quantitative Imaging of the Human Eardrum *in-vivo*

Daniel Ruiz-Cadalso, Jonathan O. Luiz, Jeffrey T. Cheng, and Cosme Furlong

Abstract We report the development of a digital holographic otoscope for high-resolution, quantitative imaging, providing insights into ear dynamics for improved diagnostics and treatment of hearing-related pathologies, with improved temporal stability over previously developed holographic otoscopes. This is achieved with the use of an instantaneous polarization imaging sensor, which contains a micro-array of four-pixel units of linear polarizing filters overlayed on the detectors, enabling the instantaneous recording of four phase-shifted holograms. Preliminary results of the realized holographic otoscope in the measurement of acoustically induced vibrations are demonstrated. The system is tested with artificial samples that are 5-10 mm in diameter and acoustically sensitive to the audible frequency range of humans. Single-shot holograms of the response to tonal stimuli of up to 20 kHz are recorded and computed in real-time using lensless reconstruction techniques, and vibration amplitudes of as small as 26 nm are quantified using stroboscopic imaging. The results show a significant improvement in the measurement stability of quantitative digital holographic otoscopes, promising the ability to characterize and diagnose eardrum pathologies in living subjects.

Keywords Digital holography · Eardrum · Otoscope · Polarization imager · Single-shot phase-shifting · Lensless reconstruction

Introduction

Digital holographic interferometry is a quantitative imaging method for extracting the optical phase of light and has been widely used for non-destructive testing (NDT) [1–3], measurement of micro- to nano-scale displacements [4], and vibration analysis [5, 6], among other applications and physical phenomena. As a high-resolution metrology technique, digital holography provides detailed full-field information about dynamic mechanical behaviors with sub-wavelength accuracy. However, it is highly sensitive to external disturbances [7], which introduce noise and limit its stability. Additionally, holographic imaging often faces challenges such as low imaging contrast, signal saturation on highly reflective surfaces [8], and computationally intensive post-processing that can hinder real-time applications.

Previous studies have explored the application of instantaneous phase shifting techniques [9-12] to overcome limitations associated with traditional phase-shifting digital holography. Instantaneous polarization imagers, which enable real-time phase retrieval through the acquisition of optically phase-shifted holograms in a single exposure, have proven effective in microscopy [13], nondestructive testing in aerospace applications [14], and acoustics and sound field imaging [10]. However, most implementations rely on transmission-mode imaging or highly specular reflective surfaces, where speckle noise is not significant. When applied to holography in diffuse reflection conditions, speckle noise becomes a major limitation for parallel phase shifting (PPS) [15], requiring new strategies to ensure robust phase retrieval and imaging stability.

Daniel Ruiz-Cadalso · Jonathan O. Luiz · Cosme Furlong
Center for Holographic Studies and Laser micro-mechaTronics – CHSLT, Mechanical & Materials Engineering Department, Worcester Polytechnic Institute, Worcester, MA
e-mail: daruizcadalso@wpi.edu; joluiz@wpi.edu; cfurlong@wpi.edu

Jeffrey T. Cheng · Cosme Furlong
Massachusetts Eye and Ear, Boston, MA
e-mail: tao_cheng@meei.harvard.edu; cfurlong@wpi.edu

Chi-Hung Hwang et al. (eds.), *Advancement of Optical Methods & Digital Image Correlation in Experimental Mechanics, Vol. 2*, Conference Proceedings
of the Society for Experimental Mechanics Series, https://doi.org/10.13052/9788743808282-9

This paper presents the development of a novel digital holographic otoscope utilizing an instantaneous polarization imager, designed to improve temporal stability in clinical environments. The proposed otoscope is constructed and tested on artificial samples that mimic human eardrum acoustically driven vibrations, demonstrating its capability to measure nanometer-scale displacements in real time. The results validate the effectiveness of instantaneous phase shifting methods for highly stable quantitative imaging, paving the way for future in vivo applications for diagnosing hearing-related pathologies.

Materials and Methods

Digital holography

Digital holography is an optical technique used to extract the amplitude and phase of light. In order to properly extract these parameters, digital holography uses the superposition of two unique coherent wavefronts which stem from the same light source but have each undergone diverse conditions in their respective paths. The recorded complex field, $\Gamma = Ae^{i\Phi}$, is computed using the phase-shifted holograms as, $\Gamma = (I_0 - I_\pi) + i\left(I_{3\pi/2} - I_{\pi/2}\right)$. Since Γ can be rewritten as, $A\cos\Phi + i\,A\sin\Phi$, the optical phase can be extracted by [16],

$$\Phi = \arctan\frac{I_{3\pi/2} - I_{\pi/2}}{I_0 - I_\pi} \quad . \tag{1}$$

The optical phase calculated from a single reconstructed field would yield static information, and thus, changes to the optical phase are measured interferometrically via a double exposure (DE) method. In this method, a hologram of an "undeformed" reference state is recorded and subsequently subtracted from "deformed" states of the object. The phase difference values are wrapped within $[-\pi,\ \pi]$ (mod2π). The phase can be unwrapped, and directly converted to displacements, d, by [16],

$$d = \frac{\lambda}{2\pi\left[1 + \cos\theta\right]}\text{unwrap}\left[\Delta\Phi\right] \quad , \tag{2}$$

where d is the out-of-plane displacement, λ is the wavelength of the light source, θ is the angle between illumination and observation axes, and $\text{unwrap}\left[\Delta\Phi\right]$ is the unwrapped optical phase.

Parallel phase shifting

Conventional methods require multiple phase-shifted holograms recorded over time, making them prone to external disturbances, whereas this paper employs parallel phase shifting (PPS) using linear polarizing filters on an imaging sensor to achieve instantaneous 4-step phase shifts, enhancing temporal stability by eliminating the need for multiple exposures. Figure 1 depicts the process of acquiring the four phase shifts using a polarized sensor [14]. After combining in a beam combiner, the reference and object beams are orthogonally polarized and then pass through a quarter wave plate (QWP) oriented at 45°, converting them into right-hand and left-hand circularly polarized light. The phase shifting for each beam at the polarized sensor can be described mathematically using Jones calculus. The recorded intensity becomes, $I = A + B\cos\left(\phi + 2\theta\right)$, where θ is the polarization filter angle.

Design of opto-electronic holographic otoscope

The design of the opto-electronic holographic otoscope is displayed in Figure 2. A continuous-wave single-longitudinal mode laser (Oxxius, Inc. L1C$^+$-AOM-532) generates a 200 mW beam with a center wavelength of 532 nm and an acousto-optic modulator (AOM) for stroboscopic capabilities. The beam is split into two and subsequently coupled into polarization-maintaining optical fibers. At the holographic otoscope head, the object beam is used to illuminate the sample, and the scattering field combines with the reference beam through a polarizing beam combiner. The polarization aspect of the optical combiner helps in ensuring orthogonality between each beam's polarization state and improving signal-to-noise ratios (SNR). Then, as described in Section 2.2, a rotatable QWP is placed.

Realized Holographic Otoscope

To achieve a compact and clinically viable digital holographic otoscope, the system design uses a Heine Beta 200 otoscope head, integrating key optical components while maintaining the ergonomic requirements for medical use. The setup, shown

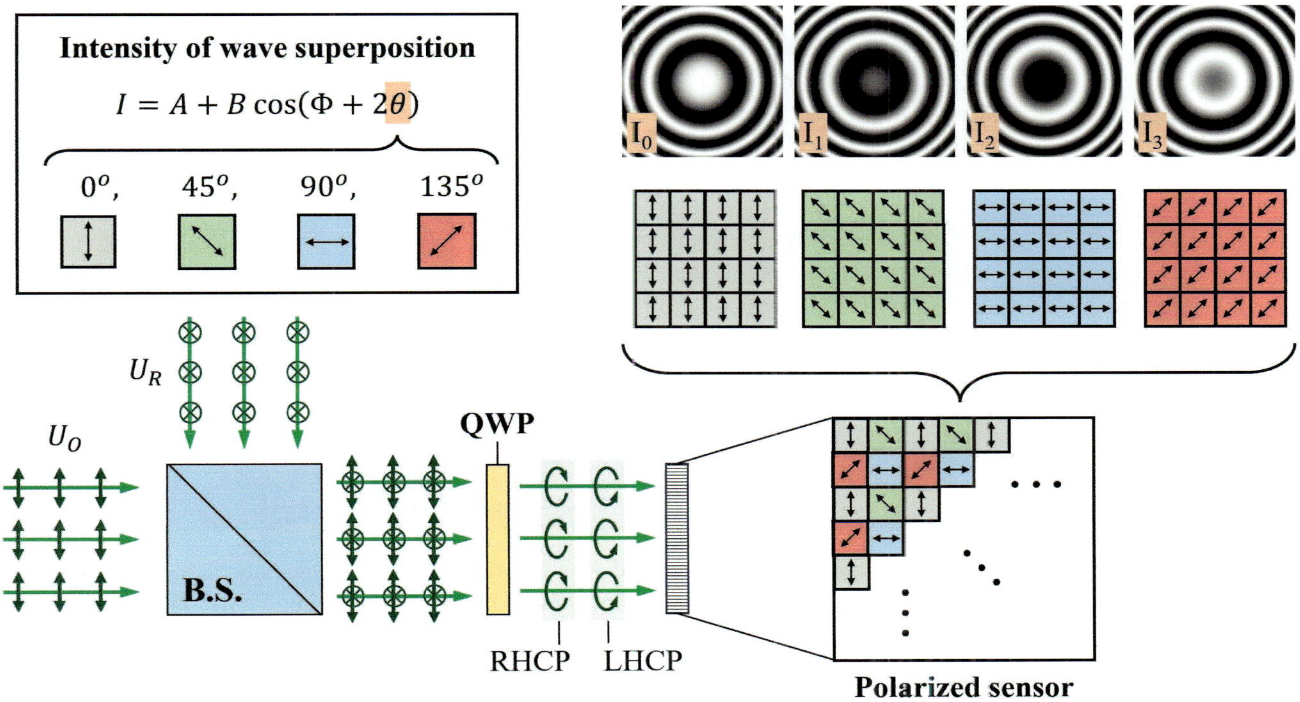

Fig. 1 Instantaneous phase shifting process by use of a polarized imaging sensor. The incoming reference and object beams are orthogonally polarized with respect to each other. With the use of a quarter waveplate (QWP), both beams are circularly polarized, one right-hand (RHCP) and the other left-hand (LHCP), which is needed for $\pi/2$-phase steps. Each step is acquired instantaneously by binning the recorded image. BS is beam splitter/combiner.

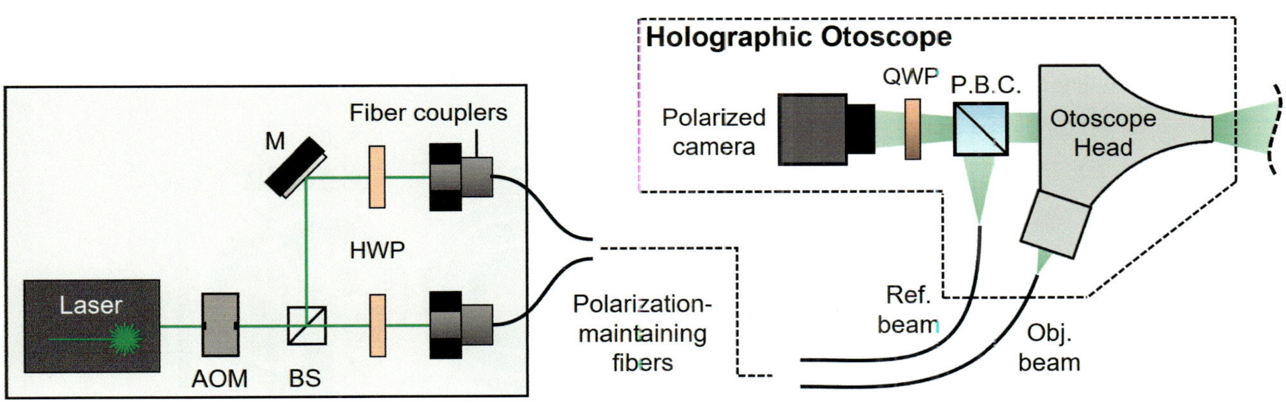

Fig. 2 Design of the opto-electronic holographic otoscope. Both interferometric beams are coupled into polarization-maintaining fibers. At the optical head, a polarizing beam combiner (PBC) is used to ensure the orthogonal polarization states. The QWP is placed between the camera and the PBC. M is mirror; HWP is half waveplate.

in Figure 3, features a 5 MP, 3.45 μm pixel, FLIR Blackfly USB polarized camera [17], with modified housing in order to fit within the confined spatial constraints of the setup. Illumination in the system is provided through the Heine otoscope's built-in optical fiber bundle, as shown in Figure 3a, which distributes light through an array of fiber cores, delivering diffuse illumination. The system's spatial resolution is validated using a high-resolution test target, shown in Figure 3b. The validated spatial resolution is approximately 18 lp/mm.

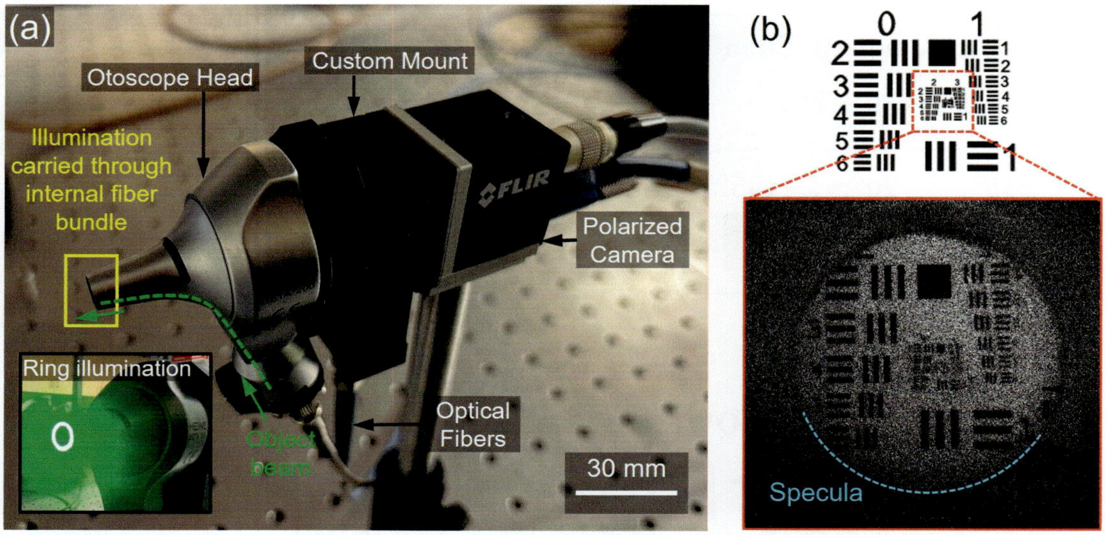

Fig. 3 Realized holographic otoscope, featuring a miniaturized design in order to achieve a clinically viable instrument: (a) realized system, which uses a Heine Beta 200, integrating key optical components while maintaining ergonomic requirements for medical use; and (b) quantitative imaging of a USAF 1951 resolution test target.

Representative Results

Acoustically induced vibrations on an artificial diaphragm

The performance of the holographic otoscope was evaluated by measuring acoustically induced vibrations of an artificial eardrum-like sample. The setup is shown in Figure 4, where the sample, which is 6 mm in diameter, is exposed to tonal stimuli within the audible frequency range of humans. Figure 4a presents the setup with the reconstructed amplitude image numerically focused on the sample. The wrapped optical phase maps describing the vibrational amplitudes were obtained for two frequencies, 3.2 kHz and 8.5 kHz, are shown in Figures 4b and 4c, respectively. The phase maps are unwrapped and converted to displacements, as described in Eq. 2, demonstrating the system's capability of capturing high-resolution acoustically induced deformations, down to 26 nm.

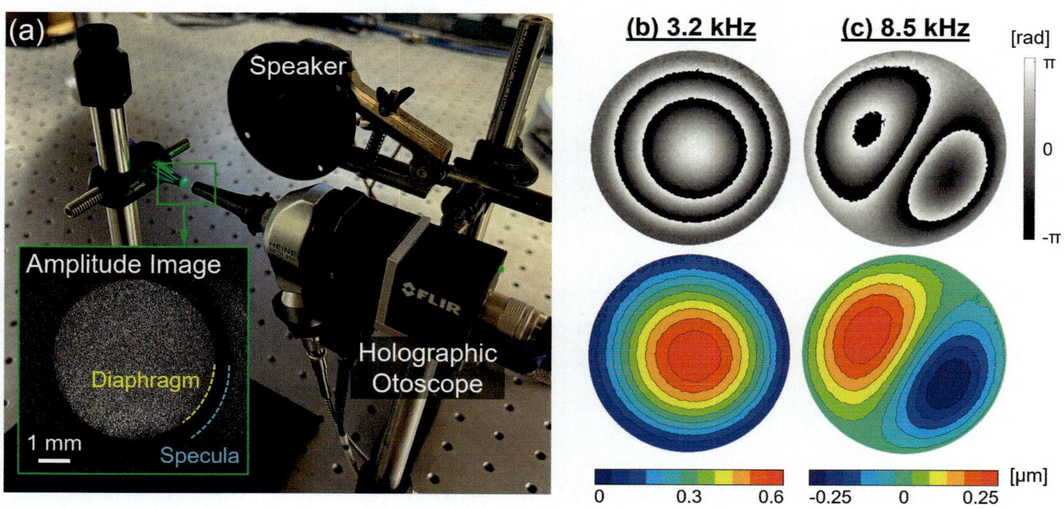

Fig. 4 Performance of the lensless digital holographic otoscope in the measurement of acoustically induced deformations: (a) setup with an artificial sample, 6 mm in diameter, a loading speaker, and the reconstructed amplitude image; (b) wrapped optical phase and amplitude displacement for 3.2 kHz; and (c) the same for 8.5 kHz.

Conclusions and Future Work

This work presents the development of a digital holographic otoscope utilizing an instantaneous polarization imager to improve measurement stability in acoustically induced eardrum vibrations. By integrating parallel phase shifting through a pixelated polarization sensor, the system effectively eliminates the need for multiple sequential exposures, significantly enhancing temporal stability and reducing motion-induced phase errors. The experimental validation on artificial eardrum-mimicking samples demonstrated the system's ability to capture real-time, single-shot holograms of high-frequency acoustic vibrations, with vibration amplitudes as small as 26 nm quantified. These findings suggest that the proposed otoscope is well-suited for noninvasive diagnostic applications in clinical environments.

Despite the promising results, several challenges remain. One major issue unique to digital holography and other laser-based optical techniques is the presence of speckle noise, which affects the accuracy of instantaneous phase shifting. While speckle size was controlled and larger than a polarization unit on the sensor, further optimization is needed to minimize degradation of phase shifting. Additionally, the miniaturization of the optical system remains a critical challenge for practical clinical deployment, as compact and ergonomic designs are necessary for routine in vivo examinations.

Future work will focus on testing the system on human subjects to assess its clinical viability for diagnosing hearing disorders and middle ear pathologies. Another key area of development will be improving the phase-shifting accuracy in the presence of speckle noise, possibly through adaptive filtering techniques or alternative polarization encoding strategies. Ultimately, the integration of this technology into clinical workflows could offer a powerful tool for quantitative, non-invasive evaluation of eardrum function, improving early diagnosis and treatment outcomes for patients with hearing impairments.

References

1. Newman, J.W., "Holographic and shearographic NDT applications in aerospace manufacturing," *Mater. Eval.*, *63*(7), 2005.
2. Ruiz-Cadalso, D. and Furlong, C., "High-resolution imaging for in-situ non-destructive testing by quantitative lensless digital holography," *Frontiers in Photonics*, *5*, 2024.
3. Ruiz-Cadalso, D. and Furlong, C., "Nondestructive Crack Detection by High-Speed Digital Holographic Interferometry and Impact-Induced Traveling Waves," *Proc., SEM 2023 Annu. Conf.*, 2023.
4. Hernández-Montes, M. del S., Mendoza-Santoyo, F., Moreno, M. F., de la Torre-Ibarra, M., Acosta, L. S. and Palacios-Ortega, N., "Macro to nano specimen measurements using photons and electrons with digital holographic interferometry: a review," *J. Eur. Opt. Soc.: Rapid Publ.*, *16*(1), p. 16, 2020.
5. Pryputniewicz, R.J., "Vibration Studies Using Heterodyne Hologram Interferometry," *SPIE Industrial Laser Interferometry II*, pp. 154–161, 1988.
6. Ruiz-Cadalso, D. and Furlong, C., "Comparative study of high-speed digital holographic interferometry and scanning laser Doppler vibrometry for modal analysis," *Proc., SEM 2023 Annu. Conf.*, 2023.
7. Sheridan, J.T., Kostuk, R.K., Gil, A.F., Wang, Y., Lu, W., Zhong, H., Tomita, Y., Neipp, C., Francés, J., Gallego, S. and Pascual, I., "Roadmap on holography," *J. Opt.*, *22*(12), 2020.
8. Bianco, V., Memmolo, P., Leo, M., Montresor, S., Distante, C., Paturzo, M., Picart, P., Javidi, B. and Ferraro, P., "Strategies for reducing speckle noise in digital holography," *Light Sci. Appl.*, *7*(1), 2018.
9. Kakue, T., Yonesaka, R., Tahara, T., Awatsuji, Y., Nishio, K., Ura, S., Kubota, T. and Matoba, O., "High-speed phase imaging by parallel phase-shifting digital holography," *Opt. Lett.*, *36*(21), 2011.
10. Ishikawa, K., Yatabe, K., Chitanont, N., Ikeda, Y., Oikawa, Y., Onuma, T., Niwa, H. and Yoshii, M., "High-speed imaging of sound using parallel phase-shifting interferometry," *Opt. Express*, *24*(12), 2016.
11. Du, Y., Li, J., Zhao, H., Zhao, Z., Fan, C., Zhou, M., Yang, X. and Zhao, R., "Accurate dynamic 3D deformation measurement based on the synchronous multiplexing of polarization and speckle metrology," *Opt. Lett.*, *48*(9), 2023.
12. Fan, C., Li, J., Du, Y., Hu, Z., Chen, H., Yang, Z., Zhang, G., Zhang, L., Zhao, Z. and Zhao, H., "Flexible dynamic quantitative phase imaging based on division of focal plane polarization imaging technique," *Opt. Express*, *31*(21), 2023.
13. Tahara, T., Ito, K., Kakue, T., Fujii, M., Shimozato, Y., Awatsuji, Y., Nishio, K., Ura, S., Kubota, T. and Matoba, O., "Parallel phase-shifting digital holographic microscopy," *Biomed. Opt. Express*, *1*(2), 2010.
14. Ruiz-Cadalso, D. and Furlong, C., "Application of instantaneous polarization imagers for quantitative optical metrology by digital holography," *Proc., SEM 2024 Annu. Conf.*, 2024.
15. Jeong, W., Son, K., Cho, J., Yang, H. and Park, N.C., "Suppression algorithm of speckle noise for parallel phase-shift digital holography," *Opt. Laser Technol.*, *112*, 2019.
16. Kreis, T., *Holographic interferometry: principles and methods*, Wiley-VCH, 1996.
17. Blackfly S USB3, *Teledyne FLIR*, 2024. https://www.flir.com/ (Accessed: February 18, 2024)